CAVALIER SAINTS
AND SINNERS

Virginia History Through a Keyhole

Also by George Holbert Tucker

Tidewater Landfalls

More Tidewater Landfalls

Norfolk Highlights (1584-1881)

Virginia Supernatural Tales

A Goodly Heritage: A History of Jane Austen's Family

The Jane Austen Companion (contributor)

CAVALIER SAINTS AND SINNERS

Virginia History Through a Keyhole

George Holbert Tucker

The Virginian-Pilot
and
The Ledger-Star

For my wife,
Elizabeth Williams Tucker,
and James Rutledge Henderson III,
the man who taught me how to write.

ACKNOWLEDGEMENTS

I would like to thank Frank Batten Jr., vice president and associate publisher of The Virginian-Pilot and The Ledger-Star, for the interest he has taken in my work; Sandra M. Rowe and James Raper, executive editor and managing editor of the papers, for not only having instituted my weekly column in Commentary but actively promoting the publication of some of the columns in book form; James Rutledge Henderson III for the tender loving care he used in editing the manuscript; Mildred ("Millie") M. Johnson for typing the final version; and Robert Mason, editor of The Virginian-Pilot from 1962 to 1978, for writing the foreword.

CONTENTS

Foreword

A friend who wrote an informal history of the Revolution had cause to reflect that maybe he was operating in the wrong century. So he switched to the Civil War, to the benefit of his reputation as an author and his wife's fondness for travel abroad. He entered his new field by reading, at an editor's suggestion, the works of Douglas Southall Freeman.

He had plowed through several hundred pages when he came to realize that Freeman's best stuff was in his footnotes. My friend quit reading the text and concentrated on the small type at the bottom of the pages for its stories and clues to more.

George Holbert Tucker would understand this. For 40 years he has been filling newspaper columns and popular books with the chaff of scholarship. The result is some of the liveliest and funniest accounts of Virginia's past that can be found, as this third collection of Tuckeriana eloquently testifies.

When, for instance, George pokes into the life and times of Henry Wriothesley (1573-1624), third Earl of Southampton, he breezes past that worthy's friendship with Shakespeare, his contributions to the Old Dominion's settlement, and even his part in a conspiracy against Queen Elizabeth I that nearly cost him his head. What George has to tell us about is not the heavy stuff of library recesses and painfully wrought academic theses, but the Earl's cat. ("...Wriothesley's cat continued to share its master's imprisonment until his release, meanwhile making serious depredations on the Tower's rats, which were notorious for their size and ferocity...")

And in George's version of President Lincoln's second visit to the Norfolk area during the Civil War, to participate in the Hampton Roads Peace Conference of February 3, 1865, a frigid day, he identifies by name every ship in the harbor and notes every landmark and public building the delegates passed or entered, and then rewards us with what he was coming to all along: a witticism. It is Mr. Lincoln's, directed in good humor at the Confederate Vice President, Alexander H. Stephens. ("Stephens, a tiny man weighing less than 90 pounds, arrived at the conference muffled in a heavy overcoat, a scarf and several shawls. Hoping to break the tension, Lincoln quipped: 'Never have I seen so small a nubbin come out of so much husk.'")

When George Tucker permits himself a glance at the more recent past — at, say, the year 1920 or so, when he was a boy in the old Berkley neighborhood across the Eastern Branch of the Elizabeth River — the reader may be sure that his memory is as reliable as his taste for

Jamestown heroics, Williamsburg indiscretions, and Norfolk visitations by the likes of Edgar Allan Poe, Oscar Wilde, Mark Twain, and Gertrude Stein. If the dust of courthouse vaults is on his cuffs, the honk of ferry boats and Chesapeake packets is in his ear, the robust songs of tent revivals — word for word — are on his tongue, and in his eyes are the explosion of fireworks over old Ocean View Park on a summer's night. ("And what fireworks they were! — not the standard pyrotechnics that are now featured throughout the Norfolk area. No, the Ocean View fireworks were truly exceptional: blazing American flags, the stars of which temporarily outshone their rivals in the heavens; gigantic portraits of George Washington as a special feature for the Fourth of July; sky-soaring replicas of the Statue of Liberty, as well as many-hued waterfalls, all bursting in air to the accompaniment of Sousa marches vehemently tooted by uniformed musicians in the bandstand.")

To receive a letter from George is to enjoy, besides his message and compliments, not exactly calligraphy but one man's undoubted improvement over the Locker Method of writing urged upon him in the fourth or fifth grade. The flourishes and curlicues of his script — and drawings too; he is an accomplished pen-and-ink artist — somehow filter through his and the typesetter's keyboards and into his printed prose. Let others enroll in the schools of Fitzgerald, Faulkner, Hemingway, and the creative-writing professors. George's style is sometimes Biblical, often Victorian, occasionally modern, even slangish, but surely his. It is consistently merry: just what it takes to express his splendid sense of the doughty, the titillating, the sumptuous, and the ridiculous.

Only in research is George canonical. Exactitude is his standard, as anyone will attest who has observed his labors in the Sargeant Memorial Room of Norfolk's Kirn Library, or in some attic where yellowing letters and records are kept in trunks and boxes (and only George is invited to come), or wherever the past and its prizes are esteemed and guarded. George Holbert Tucker is a second-cup-of-coffee historian. He also is a historian's historian.

Robert Mason
Editor of The Virginian-Pilot
1962-1978

Southern Pines, N.C.
September 1990

Part 1: "Earth's only Paradise"

Vain About Virginia

Virginia chauvinism, the deeply ingrained belief of all native-born citizens of the Old Dominion (including myself) that they and their state are superior to anyone or any place on God's green earth, had its beginning in 1606.

In that year, Michael Drayton (1563-1631) launched the Jamestown settlers on their first crossing of the Atlantic with a poetical equivalent of a bottle of champagne that he titled, "To the Virginia Voyagers."

Drayton's verses contain the line, "Virginia, Earth's only Paradise," a sentiment that created such a sensation that it has continued to flourish over the centuries like the green bay tree. It is even emblazoned today in an updated version on everything from cocktail napkins to note paper, properly embellished, of course, with cardinals and dogwood blossoms, the state's official bird and flower.

The current transformation of Drayton's plug reads: "To be a Virginian, either by birth, adoption, or even on one's mother's side, is an introduction to any state in the union, a passport to any foreign country, and a benediction from the Almighty God."

Now, that covers a lot of territory, but it is no different in sentiment from the old pro-Virginia chestnut that was so popular a few years back that it turned up on souvenirs ranging from post cards to silk-fringed sofa pillows. If you have forgotten it, here is how it began: "The roses nowhere bloom so white as in Virginia."

And as if that weren't enough, the author went on to declare that the Almighty had the Old Dominion in mind when he created heaven. If you think I am drawing a long bow, here is the ultimate quatrain:

> And I believe that happy land
> The Lord's prepared for mortal man
> Is built exactly on the plan
> Of Old Virginia.

That's laying it on with a shovel, but it will be evident from what follows that such a sentiment didn't spring up overnight. In fact, historical evidence shows Virginia chauvinism was flourishing so luxuriantly by the turn of the 19th century that John Adams, the second president of the United States, commented on it in a letter written in 1807 to Dr. Benjamin Rush, one of the signers of the Declaration of Independence.

"Virginia geese are all swans," Adams wrote rather pointedly. "Not a lad upon the High Lands (of Scotland) is more clannish than every Virginian I have ever known. They trumpet one another with the most pompous and mendacious panegyrics. The Philadelphians and New Yorkers, who are local and partial enough to themselves, are meek and modest in comparison with Virginia Old Dominionism."

Even so, criticism of that nature, particularly from anyone born north of the Mason and Dixon Line, has always been water off a duck's back to the loyal sons and daughters of the commonwealth.

Witness what William Cabell Bruce, the biographer of John Randolph of Roanoke, had to say on the subject: "No man should ever ask a man whether he was born in Virginia, because if he was, he certainly will tell you, and if he was not, he will be ashamed to admit it."

That's pretty strong, but I can add an anecdote from my own experience that will support Bruce's assertion. Once, after I had given a talk to a garden club made up of members of the Burke's Peerage of Norfolk, I was presented with a quart of

Virginia Gentleman by my appreciative hostess. When I murmured my thanks, she inquired archly, "Do you know the difference between a virgin and a Virginian?" Since I did not have a ready comeback, she smiled knowingly and answered: "Once a Virginian, always a Virginian!"

Old Dominion chauvinism even extends to those who have been long absent from their native heath, a statement that was hilariously illustrated by the great American humorist Irving S. Cobb, one of whose grandmothers was born in Virginia but moved to Kentucky with her parents as a child. Later, she married there, reared a large family and lived to a ripe old age. Except for a few short visits, she never lived again in her native state. However, until the day of her death, "home" meant only one place — the Old Dominion.

But that is not the crux of the story.

Toward the end of her life, when a stranger met her on one of her travels and inquired where she was from, she drew herself up proudly and replied, "I am a Virginian — at present stopping out in Kentucky."

Nevertheless, we sons and daughters of the Mother of States haven't always gotten away with our superior attitude. To illustrate the point, there is the lovely old story dating from the turn of the century concerning three ladies who were sitting on the front porch of a cottage in White Sulphur Springs, W. Va., one summer afternoon.

One of them, a native of Charleston, S.C., was laying it on rather thickly concerning her Low Country ancestry. This so riled the second of the trio, a Virginian, that she trumped the bragger's ace with an even more spectacular account of the derring-do of her own forebears.

When the third lady did not join in, she was asked where she was born. Her answer was a classic putdown:

"I'm from North Carolina," she purred, "the vale of humility between two peaks of conceit!"

An Earl's Best Friend

Hampton Roads, originally called South Hampton Roads, one of the world's most notable anchorages, memorializes in truncated form the title of Henry Wriothesley (1573-1624), third Earl of Southampton, a prominent member of the Virginia Company that founded Jamestown.

Wriothesley (pronounced Rizley) also was the friend and patron of Shakespeare as well as the proud owner during the earlier part of his life of what must have been one of the most remarkable cats in English history.

An outstanding member of the British nobility during the latter half of the reign of Queen Elizabeth I and the reign of her successor, King James I, Wriothesley was a Renaissance man in every sense of the word. He had a lifelong interest in the martial arts, was involved in the colonization of the New World, and was a connoisseur of ancient and contemporary literature.

Wriothesley's encouragement of many of the notable authors of his time, whose writings are now rated among the glories of English prose and poetry, has been carefully documented by scholars. Their findings reveal that he was not only an outstanding patron of the theater but a particular friend and encourager of Shakespeare.

From earliest manhood Wriothesley was keenly interested as well as actively involved in the establishment of British colonies in America, particularly in that area now known as Tidewater Virginia, and from 1609, when he became a member of the Virginia Company's council, he was one of the principal promoters of the Jamestown colony. This interest became even more notable after 1620, when he became the treasurer for the joint stock company that sponsored the settlement, all of which serves to introduce an action on his part that should always endear him to the chroniclers of Virginia's earliest beginnings.

In 1624, when the Crown took over the management of

the colony, Wriothesley was ordered to turn over the records of the Virginia Company dating from the period when he had acted as its treasurer. Knowing that these documents might be used to discredit him if he did not retain a copy, he had a transcription of the records made secretly before giving up the originals. When the royal commissioners learned that Wriothesley had retained the secretly transcribed copies, they demanded that these also be relinquished.

But Wriothesley flouted the order, saying that he would as soon part with the title deeds of his land as part with the manuscript in his possession, since he regarded it as evidence of his honorable service during the time he was treasurer of the Virginia Company.

Fortunately, Wriothesley was powerful enough to get away with his defiance, and his copy of the records (the originals of which have since disappeared) remained in his possession. After the death of Wriothesley's son, the fourth earl, the precious manuscript volumes were purchased from the executors of his estate by Colonel William Byrd of Westover, Virginia's outstanding early eighteenth century citizen, who happened to be in England at that time. Subsequently the records were owned by Thomas Jefferson, from whom they passed to the Library of Congress, where, in 1906, they were finally carefully edited and published.

These facts are interesting from a scholarly standpoint, but the story of Wriothesley's unusual cat is even more fascinating from a human-interest angle.

In 1601, when he was 28, Wriothesley became involved in the conspiracy headed by the Earl of Essex against Queen Elizabeth and was condemned to death. The sentence was later commuted to life imprisonment, but Wriothesley was granted a full pardon and was released by James I in 1603.

Meanwhile, the earl had a handsome black and white cat of which he was inordinately fond, and when he was confined in the Tower of London the cat was left behind at Wriothesley's London residence. Apparently the cat missed its master, for according to Thomas Pennant's "Of London," published in 1790, Wriothesley "was surprised by a visit from his favorite cat, which had found its way to the Tower, and, as tradition says, reached its master by descending the chimney of his apartment."

Wriothesley's cat continued to share its master's imprisonment until his release, meanwhile making serious depredations on the Tower's rats, which were notorious for their size and ferocity. In appreciation, Wriothesley had the faithful animal's likeness included prominently in a still-surviving portrait of himself that was painted while he was a prisoner in the Tower.

Bad "Queen Jamie"

James I (1566-1624), namesake of Jamestown, England's first permanent New World settlement, was one of the most enigmatic monarchs ever to occupy the British throne. Physically unattractive, as well as insanely obsessed with the doctrine of the divine right of kings, James was completely lacking in the magisterial qualities which, combined with an empathy for people in general, had distinguished his great predecessor, Queen Elizabeth I.

In addition to regarding himself as God's anointed, James' deficiencies included fancying himself a second Solomon in wisdom, and believing the type of homosexuality he practiced was an imperial vice, thereby removing him from the censure leveled at other less fortunate commoners who chose that type of sexual expression.

In commenting on James' intellectual pretensions, William Stith, the 18th century Virginia historian, wrote: "For he had been bred up under Buchanan, one of the brightest geniuses and most accomplished scholars of that age, who had given him Greek and Latin in great waste and profusion, but it was not in his power to give him good sense. That is the gift of God and nature alone, and it is not to be taught; and Greek and Latin without it only cumber and overload a weak head, and often render the fool more abundantly foolish."

As for James' homosexual activities, which can be found in any modern biography of the king, they were well known before he left beggarly Scotland to become the first male to sit on the British throne in half a century.

Prior to becoming Elizabeth's successor, James was frequently referred to snidely as "la reine Jacquette," or "Queen Jamie," in sophisticated circles at the various European courts.

After his arrival in England, accompanied by his male favorite of the moment who was subsequently replaced by other *mignons,* culminating with the infamous George Villiers, Duke of Buckingham, an anonymous court wit embalmed the situation in the following quatrain:

> While Elizabeth was England's king,
> That dreadful name through Spain did ring;
> How altered is the case — ad sa' me!
> These juggling days of gude queen Jamie!

Meanwhile, to ensure the legitimate succession of his family, James had put aside his repugnance to women in general and had married Anne of Denmark, a woman equally silly as himself, by whom he had three children whose names have been embalmed in Virginia's history and geography. Cape Henry and Cape Charles were named by the earliest colonists for Prince Henry and Prince Charles Stuart, whose names are also preserved in Henrico and Charles City counties. Norfolk's Elizabeth River was named for James' eldest daughter, Elizabeth, at whose nuptials Shakespeare's *The Tempest* received one of its earliest performances. As for James himself, he is also remembered throughout the Old Dominion as the monarch for whom Jamestown, the James River and James City County were named.

Once his line of legitimate succession was established, James resumed his homosexual dalliance, while his queen, who lived separately from him, devoted the rest of her life to staging a series or elaborate court theatricals that placed a heavy strain on the royal purse.

It was at one of these entertainments, a performance of Ben Jonson's Twelfth Night masque, *The Vision of Delight,* on January 18, 1617, that Pocahontas, then visiting England, was an honored guest. On that occasion, the Indian princess was graciously received by Queen Anne, while James, acting the jackass as usual, made a scene, declaring that John Rolfe should have secured his permission before marrying into a royal family — even though the bride's family was only Indian royalty.

Apart from his pretensions to learning, which gained him the double-edged compliment of being "the wisest fool in Christendom," James had other personal quirks that made him an unlikely progenitor of Virginia's popular representative government of today. As anyone with the slightest knowledge of Old Dominion history already knows, the first legislative assembly in the New World convened at Jamestown in 1619, five years prior to the king's death in 1624. Since he regarded himself as God's sole arbiter in English politics, James was an archenemy of parliaments of any kind, even having gone so far on one occasion as to remark, "I am surprised that my ancestors would have permitted such an institution to come into existence."

It is therefore ironic that the foundations for American representative government of today were laid in far-off Virginia during James' reactionary reign. Even so, according to *Virginia: The New Dominion* by Virginius Dabney, "Virginia's representative government continued to be opposed by James I, and later by his son, Charles I, and it was not until 1639 that the royal imprimatur was placed on Virginia's House of Burgesses and council as continuing legislative arms of the colonial period."

As for the role James played in the creation of what is popularly known as the King James Version of the Bible, he had practically nothing to do with that great monument of Jacobean prose which has preserved his name for posterity. The King James Version, also referred to as the Authorized Version, was actually produced by some 47 scholars only at the suggestion of the king and was a by-product of the Hampton Court Conference which he convened primarily to regulate the English Church.

James' stand on tobacco was much more active, however, and his *Counterblaste to Tobacco* anticipated by centuries the current crusade against smoking.

To end on a bright note, it is comforting to learn that James, despite his inclination to learned pronouncements, could occasionally give a trying situation a witty twist. Once when he was on a visit to Lumley Castle, he was received by the dean of Durham Cathedral who expatiated at great length on the antiquity of the Lumley pedigree. When he was unable to tolerate the dean's prosings any longer, James abruptly interrupted his guide. Addressing the cleric with a broad Scottish brogue, a habit of speech he never overcame, he quipped, "Oh, mon, gang na farther; let me digest the knowledge I have gained, for I did na ken Adam's name was Lumley!"

Spies for Spain

The intrigues of international espionage that continue to surface throughout the Hampton Roads area are latter-day manifestations of Virginia-based spying activities dating back to the establishment of the Old Dominion.

England's colonial ambitions were regarded with suspicion by Spain from the time Sir Walter Raleigh attempted to establish a settlement on the Outer Banks of North Carolina during the late 16th century. The Spanish maintained that the site where Raleigh's efforts eventually came to grief was a part of their North American empire which embraced the vast territory ranging northward from the present state of Florida to the land surrounding the Bahia de Santa Maria, now known as the Chesapeake Bay. The failure of Raleigh's colonial attempts quieted matters for a brief period, but when the Virginia venture which finally resulted in the establishment of Jamestown materialized, Philip III of Spain became increasingly concerned.

Formal protests made by the Spanish ambassador to the court of James I proved futile, but Philip's representative in London was not discouraged. Recent research in the Spanish archives proves conclusively that Captain George Kendall, an English Catholic pretending to be a Protestant, became one of the ambassador's willing tools in connection with the Virginia enterprise, both in England and later at Jamestown.

Kendall was an old hand at cloak-and-dagger dealings as well as a successful carrier of water on both shoulders. Earlier, while operating as a spy in London and on the European continent for His Catholic Majesty of Spain, he had also engaged in espionage for the English in the service of Sir Robert Cecil, the British secretary of state. Kendall sailed for Virginia with the first Jamestown settlers in December 1606, and later was named as one of the original councilors of the new colony. Meanwhile, he kept tabs on the progress of England's tentative colonial expansion. When matters began to go from bad to worse, he plotted with the sailors of the *Discovery*, the pinnace Captain Christopher Newport had left in Virginia when he sailed for England in June 1607, to run off to Spain to inform Philip III of the sorry plight of the Virginia experiment.

The plot was revealed by James Read, the Jamestown blacksmith, and when Kendall attempted to escape in the *Discovery* he was stopped by the guns of the fort. Tried and condemned as a secret agent, Kendall was executed by a firing squad late in 1607, the first case of capital punishment in Virginia.

Kendall's unsuccessful attempt at espionage did not deter Philip III from making further essays to learn what was going on at Jamestown. At his order, a Spanish vessel sailed from Florida to Virginia on a reconnaissance mission in 1609. When the captain detected what he believed to be an English man-of-war anchored in Hampton Roads, however, he turned back, only to be wrecked in a hurricane, an English account of which later provided Shakespeare with some of the storm imagery for the first act of *The Tempest*.

Undeterred, Philip III made another attempt to ascertain what the English were up to. Although the findings of his agents eventually provided him with firsthand information, they did not ultimately thwart England's colonial ambitions.

Early in 1611, three trusted secret agents were sent by the Spanish monarch to Virginia with instructions to permit themselves to be captured by the English. Once that took place, and providing they were not hanged, they were enjoined to spy on what was afoot along the James River and report their findings to the Spanish ambassador in London for eventual transmission to Philip III in Madrid.

The three men chosen for the Virginia espionage effort were Don Diego de Molina, a grandee of Spain; Ensign Marco Antonio Perez; and Francis Lymbry, a skilled and experienced English-born navigator. Lymbry not only had defected to the Spanish service many years earlier, but had also served as one of the chief pilots of the Invincible Armada when it sailed northward to eventual defeat and destruction in 1588.

Sailing from Lisbon, Portugal, to Cuba in April 1611, the three spies conferred briefly with the Spanish governor in Havana, after which they embarked in a caravel for Virginia, arriving off what is now known as Old Point Comfort in June 1611. Discovering a crude fortification there, which turned out to be Fort Algernon, the first bastion to occupy the site on which Fort Monroe now stands, the men had themselves rowed ashore in the caravel's longboat. On the beach the spies and the oarsmen were immediately arrested by the captain of the fort.

Pretending to be Spanish sailors in search of a lost ammunition ship, the spies asked for a pilot to assist the captain of the caravel to negotiate the treacherous shoals of Hampton Roads. At that point, Captain John Clark, a Virginia Company pilot who had only recently arrived in the colony, volunteered to return in the longboat to the caravel to assist the captain. His kindness was exactly what the spies had hoped would take place, for no sooner had Clark climbed aboard the caravel than he was made a prisoner and the ship set sail for Havana.

Meanwhile, Molina, Perez and Lymbry were taken up the river to Jamestown to be interrogated by Sir Thomas Dale, the high marshal and acting governor of the Virginia colony, who would have hanged them had he not been tricked into believing they were merely Spaniards in search of a lost ship. From then on until Dale learned their true identity, the three spies circulated freely at Jamestown, during which time they transmitted the results of their underhanded activities in code to the Spanish ambassador in London. The messages, some of which still exist, were hidden in coils of rope aboard England-bound vessels or were secreted between the double soles of shoes or boots worn by officers or sailors aboard the same ships who took the risk of conveying the information to London, knowing their efforts would be handsomely rewarded.

Although many of the observations transmitted by Molina and his confederates were invaluable to Philip III, they also reflected the increasing strength and prosperity of the Virginia colony. This temporarily discouraged further Spanish attempts to wipe out the Virginia settlement.

In the meantime, Clark, the Virginia Company pilot who had been kidnapped by the captain of the caravel, was grilled by the Spanish governor in Havana, then sent to Spain for further questioning. His greatly exaggerated reports concerning the strength of the Jamestown settlement, together with the less detailed information transmitted by Molina and his associates, is believed to have eventually deterred Philip III from ordering an all-out attack on the Jamestown colony.

Finally, when Dale learned the true mission of Molina, Perez and Lymbry from London, he imprisoned them in a ship riding at anchor at Jamestown. Later, after several years of negotiation, Clark was exchanged for Molina who was brought to England by Dale in 1616 in the same ship in which Pocahontas, her husband, John Rolfe, and their son, Thomas Rolfe, were passengers.

Perez, in the meantime, had died in prison at Jamestown, while Lymbry, who was also a passenger in Dale's ship, was hanged within sight of the English coast, presumably because of his earlier defection to the Spanish cause.

Clark, who had been nabbed by the Spanish in 1611 after they landed Molina and his confederates at Fort Algernon, lived to play an even more important role in American history. Back in London after five years of imprisonment in Cuba and Spain, he re-entered the service of the Virginia Company. Later, he was hired by Captain Christopher Jones, the skipper of the *Mayflower*, to pilot the Pilgrims' ship to the New World in 1620. After that epoch-making voyage, Clark returned to Virginia, where he died in April 1623 at the age of 47.

John Pory: Ink and Booze

John Pory (1572-1636), America's first known news correspondent and the speaker of the first Virginia assembly that convened at Jamestown in 1619, liked his liquor potent and plentiful, an addiction many of his successors have delighted in emulating. Even so, Pory's craving for strong drink did not alter the fact that his parliamentary expertise was a major factor in launching the first legislative body in English America, a group that laid the foundation for popular representative government in the United States.

Fortunately, Pory's detailed manuscript account of the proceedings, which was long believed lost, was discovered in 1853 in the Public Records Office in London by Conway Robinson, the Virginia historian. Four years later, George Bancroft, the celebrated chronicler of America's genesis, had a copy made which he published the same year in the *Collections of the New York Historical Society.* From that and other contemporary documents, historians have been able to write authoritatively concerning the six-day legislative session which deliberated in hot and humid weather from July 30 to August 4, 1619, during which time one of the delegates died.

The details of the meeting, which was attended by 20 delegates and six councilors presided over by the governor, Sir George Yeardley, are readily available in numerous accounts of American legislative history. As Pory's background and parliamentary skill which led to the success of the session are little known, however, it is time to highlight his role in history.

Born at Butters Hall in Thompson, a village in the fen country of Norfolk County, England, Pory came from a well-connected if not wealthy country family. His first cousin, Temperance Flowerdew, became the wife of Sir George Yeardley, who was later governor of Virginia and who was also primarily responsible for Pory's being at Jamestown when the 1619 assembly convened.

In the year of the Armada (1588), 16-year-old Pory matriculated at Gonville and Caius College, Cambridge, from which he received a bachelor of arts degree in 1592 and a master of arts degree in 1595. After that he remained for a time at the college, teaching Greek and mastering other languages.

In 1597 he began a period of intensive study under the Reverend Richard Hakluyt, the great Elizabethan and Jacobean geographer and historian, during which time he helped his mentor prepare the last volume of *Hakluyt's Voyages,* a seminal work that played an important role in the settlement of the North American continent.

In 1600, Pory brought out a volume of his own, an English translation of *A Geographical Historie of Africa, Written in Arabicke and Italian* by a black historian, Leo Africanus, which brought him to the attention of his adventure-minded contemporaries.

When James I convened his first parliament in 1605, Pory was elected to the House of Commons by the borough of Bridgewater in Somerset and served in that particular parliament until it was dissolved by the king in 1611. Meanwhile, Oxford University awarded Pory the degree of master of arts in April 1610 in recognition of "the reputation of his learning, and his skill in the modern languages."

After losing his seat in parliament, Pory became what was known in pre-newspaper days as a "letter writer" for several important noblemen. Since he continued this activity during his stay in Virginia, he is regarded as the primary ancestor of today's American newspaper reporters, while the accounts which he sent back to England concerning the then primitive conditions in Virginia constitute an invaluable source for American historians.

As a chronicler of current events and gossip before coming to Virginia, Pory visited France, Italy and even Constantinople, from which places (and also from London after his return) he sent pithy news letters to his patrons. These reports, which generally were dispatched at intervals of a week, were filled with comments on events as varied as the doings of princes, Ben Jonson's latest masques (Pory was a personal friend of Jonson), and the beheading of Sir Walter Raleigh. The grisly account Pory wrote of that execution suggests that he occupied a front row seat.

Despite his abilities, Pory's fondness for "the pot" kept him irregularly employed. As a result, when his kinsman, Yeardley, sailed for Virginia as governor late in 1618, he brought along Pory to serve as secretary of the colony for a three-year term, trusting that the change of scenery might curb his thirst for "the custom of strong potations." That the sea change did not alter Pory's bibulousness is a matter of record, for temptation was just as strong at Jamestown as it was in London even though the supply of strong drink in Virginia was less plentiful.

Even so, when the first assembly convened in 1619 in the "Quire of the Churche," Pory was appointed its first speaker, and on the final day of the session the members of the assembly voted him a commendation for his "great paines and labour." While in Virginia, Pory, who was also a member of the governor's council, took time out occasionally from his addiction to the bottle to promote the economic development of the colony. When his three-year term as secretary was up, however, he was happy to return to England, where his favorite tipples were in more abundant supply.

Pory made one more trip to Virginia in 1623 before settling in Lincolnshire, where he died in 1636 at the well-pickled age of 64. His estate, such as it was, was administered by his twin sister, Mary, and his will contained one clause that connects him to the present.

Pory left three acres of land to the churchwardens of his parish with the provision that two "Commemorative Sermons" be preached every year thereafter in his memory. The church at Sutton St. Edmond, Lincolnshire, still holds Pory's land, and it is good to know that the rector of the parish still keeps his memory green by preaching the two requested sermons annually.

Golden Age of Piracy

One of the Old Dominion's most fascinating offbeat yarns — the story of a born-again pirate and his former companion in crime — is chronicled in detail in volume one of the *Executive Journals of the Council of Colonial Virginia*, edited by H.R. McIlwaine, and published by the Virginia State Library in 1925.

Although omitted from history textbooks currently used in Virginia's public schools, buccaneering was associated with the Jamestown colony from its beginning.

As early as February 1609, Pedro de Zuniga, the Spanish ambassador to the court of James I, warned Philip III of Spain concerning the piratical intentions of many of those who founded the first permanent English toehold in the New World. "They have proposed," he cautioned, "that all the pirates who are out of this kingdom will be pardoned by the King if they resort there (Virginia), and the place is so perfect (as they say) for piratical excursions that Your Majesty will not be able to bring silver from the Indies without finding a very good obstacle there and that they will ruin the trade of Your Majesty's vessels, for that is the purpose of their going (there)."

So much for an early evaluation of many who left England to settle in Virginia during the 17th century, an estimate which can easily be corroborated from the writings of impartial historians who quote contemporary records to prove that many of those who are today regarded as Virginia ancestral icons were not averse to a little plain or fancy freebooting. To cite one notable example, Captain Christopher Newport, the "admiral" who brought the first settlers to Jamestown in 1607, was only too willing to line his pockets with Spanish or Portuguese gold obtained by piratical practices.

That being the case, the 17th century, which has been called the Golden Age of Piracy by many chroniclers, is replete with numerous examples of Jolly Roger activities engaged in by

Virginians and outsiders, all of which returns us to the case of the born-again pirate and his picaroon pal mentioned earlier.

In June 1682, a pirate ship sailed through the Virginia capes and made its way up the Chesapeake Bay as far as the mouth of the York River. Feeling it would be dangerous to try to elude the guns of the fort at Tyndall's (now Gloucester) Point, the captain, whose name has not been preserved, ordered his ship anchored downstream. He then dispatched several boats manned by strongly armed crews up the river with orders to plunder any prosperous estates they could spot. Landing at the plantations of Mrs. Rebecca Leake and John Williams, both wealthy Gloucester County residents, the pirates looted their homes and carried away a considerable quantity of goods, money and plate.

Outraged by the raid, the Virginia Council expressed its concern by issuing a warning "that ye Pyrate doth still continue roving within ye Capes, with intent to commit and perpartrate ye like villanies and robberies on some other (of) the Inhabitants of this Colony, or that ye s(ai)d Pyrate waites with expectation to take small vessels, sloops & shallops, as they come in and out of this Colony."

The council then appointed Colonel William Cole, one of its members, to head an expedition to bring the freebooters to heel. Before Cole could accomplish this, however, the pirates departed for the open Atlantic again. Their escape was but temporary, for the gang turned up shortly afterward in Rhode Island where five of the crew were captured and sent back to Virginia that "they might have their tryalls where they had perpetrated such villanyes."

Upon their arrival in the Old Dominion, the five buccaneers were "well loaden with Irons" and committed to the Middlesex County jail. Despite being heavily shackled, however, the rogues soon escaped. An intensive manhunt was launched but only two of the escapees, William Harrison and John Manly, were recaptured and marched off to Jamestown to await trial.

Shortly thereafter, the General Court of Virginia declared Harrison and Manly guilty of the crime of piracy and on November 28, 1682, the night before they were to be executed, they petitioned the lieutenant governor, Sir Henry Chicheley, for a two-day reprieve since one of them (which one is not indicated) had repented of his sins and wished to be baptized. The reprieve was granted and the baptism was performed, after which a warrant for the execution of the two rogues was sent to the hangman on December 8, with strict instructions that they were to be strung up the next morning.

Harrison and Manly proved to be smarter than their captors, however, for that night they not only freed themselves of their manacles, they also removed two iron bars from their cell window and escaped. When their informal departure was discovered a hue and cry was sent up for their recapture, but to no effect, all of which brings us to the zaniest part of the story.

Three nights later, the born-again fugitive from justice and his fellow rogue crawled back into the same cell through the window from which they had made their escape. When morning dawned, they sent for the flabbergasted sheriff whom they greeted with "Cheerfull Countenances" adding that they had "prepared themselves for Death and Came willingly to Submitt to ye sentence thereof."

The unprecedented conduct of the two Prodigal Sons "so wrought upon the hearts of many well Disposed Christians" at Jamestown, some of whom are known to have been as knavish as the two pirates, "that several Petitions were Presented to ye Lt Governr for Reprieve." Later, Lord Howard of Effingham, the royal governor, was instructed by the Lords Commissioners of Trade and Plantations to pardon Harrison and Manly provided they would never revert to buccaneering but would settle down as respectable citizens of the Old Dominion. Presumably this took place and the two former freebooters and their progeny joined the ranks of the First Families of Virginia.

Hapless William Carver

The picaresque career of Captain William Carver, the English master mariner who originally owned the land on which downtown Portsmouth was built, is the area's only known link with Bacon's Rebellion, the uprising led by Nathaniel Bacon against the royal government of Virginia.

Before concentrating on Carver's role in the rebellion that cost him his life, it might be a good idea to provide a few details concerning the revolt itself which threw the Old Dominion into turmoil between May and October 1676.

Bacon's Rebellion took its name from its leader, an impetuous young planter who had arrived in Virginia in 1674 after having been involved in a scheme to defraud a fellow Britisher. It was basically a populist revolt brought on by high taxes, the uncertain price of tobacco (the colony's chief money crop), resentment against Sir William Berkeley, the royal governor, for special privileges granted to his cronies, and the failure of Berkeley and his council to adequately defend the frontiers of the colony against increasingly savage Indian attacks.

The rebellion collapsed after Bacon's untimely death and Berkeley wreaked vengeance on Bacon's followers until Charles II recalled him to England, where he died in 1677. Meanwhile, the Virginia colony was left in shambles, and it was not until many years later that even a semblance of peace and prosperity was restored.

To return to Captain William Carver, the Norfolk area's only known link with the upheaval, nothing has ever been discovered concerning his early career other than that he was one of those "that go down to the sea in ships; and occupy their business in great waters." Before his death, however, Carver, who was described by a contemporary as "a valiant, stout seaman," served as a justice and sheriff of Lower Norfolk County (now the City of Chesapeake), acted as surveyor of the Southern and Eastern branches of the Elizabeth River, and represented the county in the House of Burgesses.

Twelve years before the rebellion, on September 16, 1664, Carver patented a tract of 180 acres of land on which downtown Portsmouth now stands. Later, in 1672, he killed a man, but the jury adjudged him to be temporarily insane and he was acquitted.

At the outbreak of Bacon's Rebellion, according to a contemporary narrative, "he was resolved to adventure his old Bones against the Indian Rogues," after which he joined the forces in revolt against the royal governor. After Bacon's forces had burned Jamestown in September 1676, following Berkeley's flight to the Virginia Eastern Shore, Bacon dispatched Giles Bland and Carver, two of his staunchest supporters, with 300 men to capture the ships then anchored in the James River.

Three vessels were taken, including the *Rebecca*, commanded by Captain Thomas Larrimore, a Berkeley follower, who was unwisely permitted to remain master of his ship after he claimed to have switched to the Bacon camp.

After the three captured ships were outfitted with ordnance from the Jamestown fort, Bland and Carver set sail across the Chesapeake Bay with intention of capturing Berkeley dead or alive. Upon their arrival in Eastern Shore waters, Berkeley, who was staying at Arlington, the Custis estate in Northampton County, asked Carver to come ashore for a parley, but Carver would not go until he had received the governor's written assurance of his safety. When this arrived, Carver left Bland in charge of the *Rebecca* and went ashore with a picked band of his most trusted followers, "where he was Caress'd with wine, etc. and large promises, if he would forsake Bacon, resigne his Ship and joine with him; to all which he Answer'd that if he served the Devill he would be true to his Trust, but that He was Resolved to go home and live quiet."

In the meantime, unknown to Carver, a letter from Captain Larrimore had been secretly delivered to Berkeley in which Larrimore offered to betray the *Rebecca* into the governor's hands if Berkeley would send a party of well-armed men to his ship to aid in the capture. Encouraged by this turn of events, Berkeley, "assisted by the juice of the grape," delayed Carver at Arlington. Meanwhile, a group of the governor's followers sallied forth from a nearby creek and rowed toward the vessel.

Captain Larrimore had taken the precaution of locking up the rebels' arms, and when Berkeley's men rowed under the *Rebecca's* stern "those in the Boat Slipt Nimbly in at the Gun Room Ports with Pistols etc. when one Couragious Gentleman ran up to the Deck and Clapt a Pistoll to Blands Breast, Saying you are my Prisoner...." According to *A true Narrative of the Late Rebellion in Virginia by the Royal Commissioners, 1677*, this is how Carver was captured:

"...Soone after Carver parting with the Governor rowes on Board, they permitt the Boat to come so neere as they might fire directly downe upon her, and soe they also commanded Carver on Board and secur'd him. When he saw this surprize he storm'd, tore his hair off (i.e., his peruke) and curst, and exclaim'd at the cowardice of Bland that had betray'd and lost all their designes."

Carver was hanged by Berkeley's orders a few days later and his estate was confiscated in January 1677. The acreage, with additions, was regranted in 1716 to Colonel William Craford, who founded the town of Portsmouth in 1752.

First Fidos of Virginia

Anyone aspiring to a perch on the upper rungs of the American social ladder is only too anxious to add the three genealogically important initials, FFV, signifying descent from the First Families of Virginia, to his list of blue-blooded credentials.

But there is a similar, lesser known and even more exclusive canine contingent, also entitled to be called FFVs (i.e., First Fidos of Virginia), that takes precedence over the snootier human group, most of whose ancestors arrived in the Old Dominion much later than the fist dogs that scampered ashore at Jamestown from 1607 onward.

To be more specific, although only fragmentary passenger lists survive of those early Virginia colonists who braved the Atlantic between 1607 and 1610 (few of whom left descendants), it is definitely known that there were dogs of several English breeds on many of the tiny ships that transported their masters to the New World. What is more, being hardier than their owners, the dogs survived, bred and became the progenitors of some of the oldest breeds now listed in the blue book of the American Kennel Club.

That there were dogs at Jamestown during the first years of the settlement is evident from two contemporary references. In the spring of 1608, when Captain John Smith was on a visit to Powhatan, he presented the Indian "emperor" with a suit of red woolen cloth, a white greyhound and a sugarloaf hat. Later, George Percy, in describing the terrible "Starving Time" of 1608-09, wrote in his *Trewe Relation:*

Then haveinge fed upon Horses, and other beastes as long as they lasted we were glad to make shifte with vermine as doggs, Catts, Ratts, and myce.

All of which was reason enough for any self-protecting canine to defect to the Indians, where it would have received plenty to eat rather than winding up on a roasting spit over a fire at Jamestown.

Percy's grisly jotting indicate that the dog population (pardon me, the First Fidos of Virginia) was considerably depleted during the time he described. But by 1619, the colonists were again well supplied with canines from across the Atlantic. This is proved by one of the acts of the first legislative assembly at Jamestown, dated August 4, 1619, which reads:

That no man do sell or give any of the greater howes (hoes) to the Indians, or any English dog of Quality, as mastiv (mastiff) greyhound, bloodhounde, land or water spaniel, or any other dog or bitche whatsoever of the English race, upon paine of forfeiting 5s sterling to the publique use of the Incorporation where he now dwelleth.

The dogs mentioned in this act constitute a catalog of virtually every blooded canine breed then common in England and Virginia. The mention of mastiffs is of particular interest as they played an important role in a controversy between idealism and practicality in early Virginia.

This is evident from an account written by John Pory, secretary of Virginia, and published in Captain John Smith's *General History*. In it, Pory related how George Thorpe, a saintly but misguided dreamer who gave up a posh job at the British court to come to Virginia to christianize the Indians, incurred the wrath of many of the more realistic-minded settlers for having their mastiffs shot.

Pory's account reads:

He (Thorpe) thought nothing too deare for them (the Indians), he never denied them anything; insomuch when they complained that our Mastives did feare them, he caused some of them to be killed in their presence, to the great displeasure of the owners, and would have had all the rest guelt (castrated) to make them milder, might he have had his will.

Ironically, Thorpe, who not only did everything he could to make Christianity attractive to the Indians but also is known to have distilled the first corn liquor in what is now the United States, was one of the first victims of the bloody Indian massacre of 1622.

Space does not permit the mention of the many references to the First Fidos of Virginia that occur in the early 17th century colonial records, but there is one that will appeal to all lovers of man's best friend, whether or not their pets are eligible for membership in the canine contingent of the FFVs.

The first case of "Love me, love my dog" in early Virginia is found in the Minutes of the Council and General Court for 1622-23. Under the date of February 4, 1622, there is an account of a free-for-all that took place at Jamestown, brought on by an unspecified breed of dog that got too intimate with the leg of a settler named Kildale. The record is so crabbedly written that it is almost impossible at this late date to untangle all the details.

That Kildale was severely bitten, however, is evident. This angered him so greatly that he "cockt his piece" and killed the offending pooch. This caused a hue and cry in which several friends of the dog's owner not only subjected Kildale to a good deal of sulfurous language, but ended up giving him a severe drubbing with several "great sticks of wood that lay at the door."

Despite his dogbite and broken head, Kildale came out on top in the scrape. Not only was the dog's owner commanded to pay his doctor's fee, but he and his cronies had to give bond that no further occurrences of the sort would disturb the public peace.

Also, one of Kildale's belaborers, who did not report before the governor at the hearing as directed, was ordered arrested and brought to Jamestown to be "laid in heels (confined to stocks) all night following" — in short, treated like a dog.

Lost Pocahontas

Over the years it has become the pious duty of countless Virginians who visit England to make a pilgrimage to St. George's Church, Gravesend, to pay tribute to Pocahontas, who was buried there in March 1617. They should have spared themselves the trouble, for even though it is a historical fact that Powhatan's "darling daughter" was buried beneath the chancel of St. George's after she died while reluctantly preparing to return to Virginia, her bones were moved and have never been found.

Even so, the claim is still being made that they are interred there, an assertion that is no doubt encouraged by officials of the church, principally because dedicated sons and daughters of the Old Dominion who visit the church annually are a source of generous contributions toward keeping it from being declared "in excess," a Britishism signifying superfluous.

Only a few years ago, G. William Whitehurst, who then represented Norfolk and Virginia Beach in Congress, came up with the pleasant but impractical suggestion that Pocahontas' remains be returned to her native Virginia. According to a Washington-dated Associated Press story that appeared in The Virginian-Pilot for November 5, 1975, Representative Whitehurst not only advocated the return by Great Britain of what might be left of the exceptional young Indian woman who figured so prominently in early Virginia, but was further quoted as saying that Pocahontas "is an important part of American history."

Now no son or daughter of the Old Dominion with even an elementary knowledge of the subject will dispute Whitehurst's estimation of Powhatan's favorite daughter, whom Captain John Smith apostrophized as the "nonpareil" of Virginia. As for his suggestion concerning the exhuming and returning of her bones to her native land, that would be a powwow of another sort. For the incontestable fact remains that there would be nothing to return, as any number of efforts over the years to locate and identify Pocahontas' remains have failed.

Only the brief highlights of Pocahontas' life need detain us here. Born about 12 years before Jamestown was settled in 1607, she was captured and held hostage by the English in 1613. Later, she "renounced publickly her countrey idolatry," was baptized with the Christian name of Rebecca, a Hebrew derivative meaning to tie or bind, married John Rolfe in 1616, and visited England, where she sickened and died in 1617 at Gravesend, a few miles down the Thames from London.

Because of the carelessness of the parish clerk at St. George's, where she was buried on March 21, 1617, in the rector's vault, one of two vaults beneath the chancel of the church, her husband's given name was recorded incorrectly in the still-existing parish register, which states: "Rebecca Wrolfe, Wyffe of Thomas Wrolfe Gent a Virginia Lady borne."

The two vaults beneath the chancel of St. George's were used for other burials during the 17th century. Later, at some unknown date, they were cleaned out, and the bones they contained, including those of Pocahontas, were deposited elsewhere.

St. George's burned in 1727 and the present Georgian edifice was built to replace the earlier Gothic structure. It was to this new church that a memorial tablet and two stained glass windows commemorating Pocahontas were presented in 1914 by the Colonial Dames of America. In 1958, a life-size bronze statue of Pocahontas, identical to the one at Jamestown, was unveiled in St. George's churchyard by Virginia Governor John S. Battle, at which time several Virginia dogwood trees were planted nearby.

To return to the problem of Pocahontas' remains, a detailed discussion of the subject can be found in *Pocahontas and Her World* by Philip L. Barbour (1969). Briefly, this is a summary of his in-depth inquiry into the matter:

The present St. George's was renovated in 1892, when a new chancel was built. While this work was in progress the two vaults from the earlier Gothic church were rediscovered. When opened they were both empty. Five years later, when a new north aisle for the church was being constructed, a large number of charred bones and skulls were turned up when the foundations were being dug. These were reburied outside the church in a private vault belonging to a family named Curd.

Still the quest for Pocahontas' remains continued. In 1907, the London Mail for July 22 published an article reporting that a skeleton had been unearthed at Gravesend which was reputed to be that of Pocahontas. However, the skull, after scientific investigation, proved to be that of a black who had been killed by a blow on the back of the head. But this did not discourage those who persisted in believing that Pocahontas' remains were still at Gravesend, and in 1923 a group was organized by the Virginia art critic, J. Page Gaston, to further investigate the matter.

Permission was obtained to open the Curd family vault in St. George's churchyard, in which the charred bones discovered when the new north aisle was built in 1897 had been deposited, in an effort to find Pocahontas' skeleton. That effort was also fruitless, for after having first exhumed the bones of pig, sheep, cat, dog, ox and rabbit, the diggers discovered the remains of at least 130 individuals, none of which could by any stretch of the imagination be connected with Pocahontas.

This should have settled the matter, but another possibility presented itself. Long before the Gaston investigation was made a gruesome story had gone the rounds in England which, had it been true, might have accounted for the absence of any material evidence of Pocahontas' remains at Gravesend. According to this yarn, Pocahontas' corpse had been stolen by body snatchers soon after her burial and taken to London where efforts to sell it to doctors for anatomical purposes were foiled. The body was reinterred in an unspecified London churchyard, after which all traces of it disappeared.

Again, this tale is apparently apocryphal, for according to Barbour it was undoubtedly a fanciful embroidery on the known fact that an Indian squaw was buried in the London churchyard of St. John Evangelist, Waterloo Road, in 1835.

Powhatan Bests Dale

During 1990 the Jamestown Settlement gallery displayed Powhatan's Mantle, Virginia's most important early Indian artifact, on loan from the Ashmolean Museum in Oxford, England. A few biographical highlights concerning its original owner are in order. At the same time, this will provide me with an opportunity to share a juicy bit of scandal that has hitherto been swept under the rug by humorless Old Dominion historians in which the wily head chieftain of the Algonquins bested one of the cruelest of the British interlopers who invaded his traditional hunting grounds. First, however, a brief resume of Powhatan's life:

Even though the English settlers referred to him as Powhatan, that was not his name. His real name was Wahunsonacock, and he was born around 1550 in the Algonquin Indian village of Powhatan near the present site of Richmond. Since Wahunsonacock is a mouthful, I'll refer to Powhatan from now on by the name by which he is known in history.

Tradition says Powhatan was a son of an Indian chieftain who had been driven northward from Florida with his followers by the Spanish, or even from the West Indies. In any event, Powhatan's father conquered five of the local Virginia tribes of his time, while his more famous son extended his sway over many others during the last quarter of the 16th century.

The resulting empire, of which Powhatan was the undisputed chief ruler, was known as the Powhatan Confederacy. At the time Jamestown was settled it consisted of 30-odd tribes and upward of 12,000 Indians who lived in more than 200 tidewater villages scattered southward from the Potomac River to the present Virginia-North Carolina line.

Crafty, ambitious and often cruel, Powhatan was nevertheless an able ruler. As the civilization which he and his subjects represented was at least a thousand years behind the more sophisticated technology that the English brought with them, however, it was only a matter of time before the Algonquin way of life would be ruthlessly exterminated.

When Jamestown was settled, Powhatan's chief village was on Purton Bay on the north side of the York River and was known as Werowocomico. It was there that Captain John Smith had his first encounter with Powhatan in either December 1607 or January 1608. Smith had been captured by the Indians. Brought before their chief ruler, he was so awed that he wrote this description of his captor's court:

"Arriving at Weromocomico, (we saw) their Emperour proudly lying upon a Bedstead a foote high, upon tenne or twelve Mattes, richly hung with mani Chaynes of great Pearles about his necke, and covered with a great Covering of Rahaughcums (raccoon skins). At his head sat a woman, at his feete another; on each side sitting uppon a Matte uppon the ground, were raunged his chiefe men on each side of the fire, tenne in ranke, and behinde them as many young women, each with great Chaynes of white Beades over their shoulders, their heades painted in redde; and Powhatan with such a grave and majestical countenance, as drave me into admiration to see such state in a naked Savage."

Smith was also impressed by Powhatan's 50 bodyguards chosen from among his tallest warriors as well as numerous concubines who constantly waited on him. As for Powhatan himself, Smith described him thus: "...of personage a tall, well proportioned man with a sower looke; his head somewhat gray, his beard so thinne that it seemeth none at all. His age neare 60, of a very able and hardy body to endure any labour."

Shrewd as he was, Powhatan missed his supreme opportunity of wiping out the English colony during the terrible Starving Time of 1609-10. This mistake, and superior English firepower, eventually spelled the doom of his people. Meanwhile, he found it necessary to abandon Werowocomico on the York River and take up a more remote post at "Orapakes" at the head of White Oak Swamp.

The move coincided with the capture of Pocahontas in 1612, and her subsequent marriage to John Rolfe two years later, both of which events took place during the time Sir Thomas Dale was high marshal and deputy governor of Virginia from 1611 to 1616, a period long remembered for Dale's brutal cruelty.

Just before sailing for Virginia in 1611, Dale had married,

but he left his wife behind in England. His celibate life in Virginia apparently became distasteful, however, for according to *A True Discourse of the Present State of Virginia,* written by Ralph Hamor and printed in London in 1615, Dale began to cast about in 1614 for a suitably lusty bed companion.

Soon after Pocahontas' marriage, and masking his lechery with a lie, claiming he intended to settle permanently in Virginia, Dale sent Hamor to Powhatan asking the latter to send him one of Pocahontas' younger sisters to be "his nearest companion, wife and bedfellow." But Powhatan was not taken in. He told Hamor the maiden Dale desired for carnal purposes had already been betrothed to one of his chieftains and sent him back to Jamestown. Since Dale returned to England in 1616, one year after Hamor's pamphlet had been printed, one can't help wondering what Lady Dale thought about this peccadillo of her husband in the far-off wilds of Virginia.

Saved by Chanco

Chanco, the Christianized Indian boy whose timely warning saved the Virginia colony from almost certain destruction in the Indian massacre of March 1622, is now almost forgotten. He deserves better treatment than he has received to date from chroniclers of the Old Dominion.

To background the events leading up to the massacre, an uneasy truce had existed between the Indians and the English settlers from the time of the marriage of Pocahontas and John Rolfe in 1614. This continued until Powhatan, Pocahontas' father and the chief ruler of the Powhatan Confederacy, died in 1618. Meanwhile, from 1607 on, those colonists who had survived the "seasoning period" and the terrible "Starving Time" of 1609-10 had made it evident that they intended to remain in Virginia to serve as a nucleus for England's first permanent overseas expansion.

For Powhatan's subjects, whom most of the arrogant English intruders regarded as barbarians and infidels, that meant a rapid loss of their traditional territories as well as the eventual obliteration of their age-old way of life. Cowed by the usurpers' more sophisticated weapons and technology, however, the Indians could only feign a friendliness for the overbearing English and hope for a leader from their own ranks who would turn their complaints into action. This desire was not long unfulfilled.

Opechancanough, Powhatan's younger brother and successor, was well aware of the desperate plight of his people, but was prevented from acting during the Peace of Pocahontas, which had been instituted by her father after her marriage to an Englishman. When Opechancanough learned belatedly that his niece, then Mrs. John Rolfe, had died in England in March 1617 while preparing to return to Virginia, he decided the time had come to secretly scuttle the humiliating truce and promote an all-out effort to drive the hated invaders from his peoples' hereditary hunting grounds.

By 1622, the year Opechancanough and his braves finally acted, the English had established themselves on small plantations and palisaded settlements from the tip of the lower Virginia Peninsula to the falls of the James River. Trusting wily Opechancanough's assurance that "sooner should the sky fall than peace be dissolved," the colonists continued with their daily dealings with the Indians, little dreaming that a plot was being perfected around the smoldering campfires that, if successful, would wipe out the colony. A friendly Indian chieftain on the Virginia Eastern Shore sent a warning to the governor at Jamestown that serious trouble was brewing, but the admonition was ignored.

In the meantime, Opechancanough's warriors visited the far-flung settlements regularly on a friendly basis, borrowed the colonists' boats to ferry their forces to strategic points from which the massacre could be more easily managed, and even slept in the houses of some of the unsuspecting settlers the night before the butchery.

Then, quite suddenly, at 8 in the morning on Good Friday, March 22, 1622, the Indians fell upon their victims on a front extending 150 miles along the James River, killing many of them with their own guns, axes and knives. By nightfall, 347 white men, women and children had been murdered, while their houses and tobacco barns had been torched by the rampaging savages. All of which brings us to the story of how Chanco, the Christianized Indian boy, risked the displeasure of his people to help his English benefactors.

Chanco, who had lived with Captain William Perry, an "ancient planter" who had come to Virginia in 1611, had been treated well by his employer, who had imparted the teachings of Christianity to his Indian servant. On the night before the massacre, Chanco was staying with Richard Pace at his plantation, "Pace's Paines," on the south side of the James River opposite Jamestown. Toward nightfall, Chanco was visited by one of his brothers, and shortly after they had gone to bed the latter informed Chanco of the plot, instructing him to murder Pace the next morning when the signal to begin the massacre was given.

According to a contemporary letter preserved in the British Library, "...it chanced in the place neare which the

Governour himselfe lived, that an Indian youth asked another Indian youth (who was baptized & served an English Gentleman of the colonie & had bin in England) If he knew, what they must do at this feast? What saith the other? Why, quoth he, we must cutt all the English Mens throats, & I hope, thou wilt cutt thy Masters."

Instead of following his brother's instructions, Chanco went to Pace and revealed the plot. Heeding Chanco's warning, Pace dressed quickly, secured his house, and rowed across the river to Jamestown "before day" to spread the alarm. Stunned by Pace's communication, the governor sent out warnings to all of the settlements within reach. As a result, according to an account of the massacre written later by Captain John Smith, thousands were saved "by this one converted Infidel."

Unfortunately, word of the impending danger could not be gotten to the outlying settlements in time, and the resulting carnage and property damage that took place the next morning came near bringing the Virginia experiment to ruin.

Chanco, who undoubtedly was regarded as a traitor by his own people, made one more appearance in recorded history. Since the letter quoted earlier stated he had already been in England, it is possible that he was one of the Indians who had accompanied Pocahontas and John Rolfe to London in 1616. Since this cannot be proved, however, it is best to stick to the following fact which, until recently, has been overlooked by writers on early Virginia history.

In April 1624, according to the minutes of the London Company, when Chanco's benefactor, Captain William Perry, was one of the petitioners sent from Virginia to England to seek relief for the colony after the massacre, he took Chanco along. On April 26, 1624, Perry brought Chanco to the attention of the directors of the company, at which time a motion was made to provide for his future maintenance "whereby to bring him up in Christianitie and some good course to live by."

What happened to Chanco after that is unknown. But even at this late date it would be a graceful gesture if the Virginia Assembly honored his memory, since his loyalty to his employer made it possible for the Old Dominion to survive the carnage of that far-off Good Friday in 1622.

John Smith, Adventurer

The colorful career of Captain John Smith did not end when he sailed for England from Jamestown in October 1609 to receive treatment for a severe gunpowder burn that nearly cost him his life. Not only did Smith, who was then 29, live for another excitement-crammed 22 years, he added further laurels to a career that had been characterized by adventure from the time he left his native Lincolnshire as a boy.

Even though Smith was unquestionably the most able administrator during the first years of the Virginia experiment, he had incurred the hatred of the upper crust drones who had come to Virginia for the sole purpose of amassing a quick fortune that would enable them to swagger in idleness for the rest of their lives. Many of these malcontents, who regarded Smith as a base-born upstart, had friends and relations in high places. Because he had forced them to work or starve while he was president of the Jamestown Council, these gallants had lodged complaints against him with the Virginia Company in London.

As a result, as soon as Smith's wound had healed sufficiently, he was called before the directors of the company to answer these accusations. The records of the proceedings no longer exist, but it is generally believed that the charges were eventually dropped. Even so, the diehards on the company's board, who had been influenced by the gossip concerning Smith's alleged harshness toward his self-styled betters while he was at Jamestown, had sufficient influence to bar him from further employment by the Virginia Company.

Never one to luxuriate in idleness, Smith obtained the patronage of a young member of the Clothworkers' Company named Marmaduke Rawdon (or Roydon), recently married to a 19-year-old heiress named Elizabeth Thorowgood who had brought him a princely dowry of 10,000 pounds sterling.

Rawdon sent Smith on an expedition to what is now the

coast of Maine and Massachusetts with instructions to discover a gold mine and to bring back a cargo of whale oil. Recalling the futile gold-grubbing mania that had infected Jamestown earlier, thwarting any attempts toward serious settlement, Smith ignored Rawdon's request. Instead, he loaded his vessels with easily-merchandised furs obtained by barter from the Indians and salted fish. Meanwhile, he explored the territory to which he gave the name "New England," the appellation it has borne since.

Smith's precise explorations resulted in a beautifully detailed map of the area published after his return to England. Like his earlier splendid chart of Virginia, Smith's New England map is so accurate that it continues, like its Virginia counterpart, to be used by archaeologists in tracking down the sites of the Indian villages that once dotted the unspoiled wilderness in both areas.

Smith reaped little pecuniary reward from his venture into North Atlantic waters except he was henceforth known as the Admiral of New England. Rawdon soon ceased to be Smith's patron when the gold mine he expected to discover did not materialize. That did not discourage Smith, who began looking around for other adventurous employment. His next patron was Sir Ferdinando Gorges, one of the organizers of the Virginia Company of Plymouth, for whom Smith made several unsuccessful attempts to return to New England, the last time being captured by French pirates. Lucky, as usual, Smith was befriended by a "Madam Chanoyes at Rochelle," who is otherwise unidentified, through whose efforts he was able to escape his captors and return to England.

Back in London, Smith had his well-known reunion with Pocahontas, who had been brought back to England with her husband and child for publicity purposes by the Virginia Company. The encounter, according to Smith, was a traumatic one for Pocahontas, who told Smith, "They (i.e., the English at Jamestown) did tell us always you were dead, and I knew no other till I came to Plymouth. Yet Powhatan did command Uttamatomakkin (i.e., one of the Indians who accompanied Pocahontas to England) to seek you, and know the truth, because your countrymen will lie much."

Meanwhile, Smith's pen had not been idle, and though he was never to return to Virginia or New England, his maps and books were highly regarded as spurs for colonial expansion. Smith even offered to accompany the Pilgrim Fathers when they set out for the New World, but they rebuffed his offer with sanctimonious cant, telling him that although his charts and writings were valuable to them, he was not a desirable companion.

Later, after the news of the Indian massacre of 1622 reached London from Virginia, Smith offered his services again to the Virginia Company, asking that it send him with a company of soldiers to the colony to punish the Indians. But Smith's enemies still had the upper hand in the Virginia Company boardroom, and he was again refused employment.

Even though they did not know it, the Pilgrim Fathers, or "Saints," as they piously referred to themselves, and the Virginia Company did posterity a favor by refusing Smith's offers. This gave him time to concentrate on his writings, and three of the books written during the last years of his life are particularly notable. Not only did Smith compile the first nautical dictionary in the English language, published in 1626-27 as *A Sea Grammar,* his *The General Historie of Virginia, New England, and the Summer Isles* (1624) and *The True Travels, Adventures and Observations of Captain John Smith in Europe, Asia, Africa and America* (1630) are among the minor classics of Anglo-American literature.

By the time *The True Travels* was published, however, Smith was nearing the end of his picaresque 51-year career. By June 20, 1631, when he made his will, the original of which turned up in a box of dusty documents in the Public Record Office in London in 1966, he was so ill he was unable to sign the document, even though he made several attempts. Although Smith was a relatively poor man, he left a fairly large library which was divided among three of his best friends. Interestingly, one of these was John Tradescant, the owner of Powhatan's Mantle recently on loan at the Jamestown Settlement from the Ashmolean Museum in Oxford, England.

Smith died the day after he made his will, leaving 20 pounds to defray the cost of his funeral and burial in St. Sepulchre's Church in London. His original gravestone was destroyed in the great London fire of 1666. Fortunately, Smith's lengthy epitaph was printed in full in Stow's *Survey of London* in 1633, and this was reengraved on a new stone in recent years and was installed over his reputed burial place. It begins with these stirring lines:

> Here lyes one conquered that hath conquered Kings.
> Subdu'd large Territories, and done things
> Which to the World impossible would seem,
> But that the Truth is held in more esteem.

That was not an unfitting tribute to a humble farmer's son from Willoughby in Lincolnshire.

Part 2: From Colony to Liberty

Perils of the Declaration

It is a miracle that the Declaration of Independence, "engrossed on parchment" between July 19 and August 2, 1776, has survived. Made available for official confirmation by John Hancock, president of the Continental Congress, on the latter date, it was signed by at least 50 delegates from the 13 former colonies. Even so, there were stragglers, for the historic document did not receive its last signature, that of Delaware's Thomas McKean, until the following year. From then on, the Declaration has experienced a checkered and frequently perilous history.

During the Revolutionary War when the British occupied Philadelphia, forcing the Continental Congress to flee for safety, the epoch-making blast against George III and his inept ministers was packed in a trunk with other important legislative papers and was taken to such places as Lancaster and York, Pa.; Annapolis, Md.; and Trenton, N.J.

When George Washington became the first president of the new nation in 1789, he insisted that the document be lodged in the office of his secretary of state, Thomas Jefferson, who also happened to be its author. Later, when the seat of government was moved from New York, the first national capital, to Philadelphia, the Declaration was dispatched to the latter place by ship.

Still later, when Washington, D.C., became the United States capital, the document was transferred there and was proudly displayed in the Executive Mansion during the presidencies of John Adams, Thomas Jefferson and James Madison.

In 1814, the Declaration had its first brush with disaster. Before the British burned what was later known as the White House, Dolley Madison, the president's spirited wife, and James Monroe, then secretary of state, hastily crammed it into a linen sack and sent it by wagon with other important state papers, to the home of a clergyman in Leesburg, Va., for safekeeping.

Returned to Washington after the Treaty of Ghent ended the War of 1812, the Declaration was stored in various government buildings. In 1820, it was turned over to the State Department, where it was kept rolled up like a scroll. In 1841, Daniel Webster, then secretary of state, felt it should be publicly displayed. At that time it was unrolled, mounted and framed.

Once that was accomplished, the Declaration was moved from Webster's office to the new Patent Office, then a part of the Department of State, where it was hung facing an uncurtained window, yellowing and fading for the next three decades.

By 1876, when the document was sent to Philadelphia to be displayed at the Centennial Exposition, it had begun to show its age; for by that time many of the signers' signatures were so faint that they could hardly be read. When the centennial closed, the Declaration was returned to the State Department, where it remained for 17 years. Fortunately, it was not rehung in its former place at the Patent Office, since that agency burned shortly after the yellowed parchment was returned from Philadelphia in 1877.

By 1894, the serious deterioration of the document began to cause so much concern that it was sealed between two plates of glass and was stored in a safe in the State, War and Navy Building. For the next 27 years it was rarely exhibited.

In 1921, a committee of experts formed to study the document reported that its condition could hardly be much worse. Despite their objection, however, it was felt that the Declaration would be a prime attraction for the Library of Congress. It was therefore taken out of hiding and sent there in a Model T Ford mail truck. It remained on exhibition in a special place in the library until the outbreak of World War II.

For fear that Washington might be subjected to enemy air attack, the Declaration was again moved on December 26, 1941. It was packed in a specially designed bronze container and traveled by Pullman railway coach with an escort of Secret Service guards to Fort Knox, Ky., where it was placed in an underground vault of the Bullion Depository.

Even though peace had not been achieved three years later, it was by then deemed safe to return the Declaration to Washington. On October 1, 1944, it was reinstalled in the Library of Congress, where it was sealed in insulating glass from which any air had been expelled. At the same time cellulose paper was placed behind the aging parchment to absorb moisture and to offset changes of temperature. To protect the document from glare, a new indirect lighting system was installed where the Declaration was displayed, while guards from the Army, Navy and Marine Corps began standing watch over it on a rotating basis.

With the completion of the National Archives Building eight years later, it was decided to make that agency the permanent caretaker of the Declaration. On December 13, 1952, it was transferred to its present home in an Army armored personnel carrier accompanied by an escort of tanks, a band and troops carrying machine guns.

Since then, Jefferson's great Declaration has been one of the most popular exhibits at the National Archives Building. Thanks to modern, sophisticated techniques, it has been beautifully restored to almost pristine condition and, together with the originals of the Constitution and the Bill of Rights, it is now housed in a bulletproof, helium-filled display case.

As an added security measure, the push of a button can send the entire display down 22 feet through the floor into a 55-ton vault of steel and reinforced concrete.

Despite these precautions, the Declaration had another narrow escape in 1986 when a crackpot wielding a claw hammer smashed the outer glass case in which it is displayed. Fortunately, the inner case and the document itself were not damaged.

Now magnificently housed in a shrinelike setting of variegated marble and gleaming bronze, the Declaration of Independence and the later seminal manifestos that resulted from the courage the original signers displayed when they put their lives on the line in 1776 are appropriately one of the stellar attractions of the national capital.

Pay them a visit the next time you are in Washington and be proud that you are an American.

Deflating the Dollar Toss

It might be good to debunk once and for all the moth-eaten tradition that George Washington threw a silver dollar across the Potomac River.

Now as anyone with good eyes and clear vision who has ever stood on the lawn of Mount Vernon knows, the Potomac at that particular point is two miles wide. It therefore goes without saying that the dollar that Washington is reputed to have tossed so cavalierly would have needed divine assistance in order to reach half that distance, much less to make it to the Maryland shore on the opposite side.

How such a yarn ever got going in the first place is a mystery, but two things are certain. One, it was hatched by someone with no knowledge of the geographical aspects of the Mount Vernon area. Two, it was apparently dreamed up by some spinner of tall tales in an effort to give the Father of Our Country the added achievement of Herculean strength.

As any admirer of the Squire of Mount Vernon is aware, there are so many wonderful things about him that his accomplishments are in no need of embellishment, even if the touching up is provided by an accomplished violator of veracity.

Proof that Washington never hurled a dollar across the Potomac, or anywhere else for that matter, has been available since 1860, when Mrs. Robert E. Lee published the memoirs of her father, George Washington Parke Custis (1781-1857). The full title of the book, in case any Doubting Thomases would like to check my facts, is *Recollections and Private Memoirs of Washington by His Adopted Son, George Washington Parke Custis*, published by J.W. Bradley of Philadelphia.

Mrs. Lee's father not only was named for George Washington but was reared by him after he was left an orphan as an infant. As young Custis was 18 at the time of Washington's death in 1799, he was therefore in the position to know a great deal concerning the intimate life of the master of Mount Vernon, and his memoirs, although written in the pompous style of his period, record many facts concerning his adoptive father that otherwise would have been lost.

Before going into the details concerning the supposed dollar-throwing episode, it might be a good idea to record a few facts concerning Washington's size and physical strength. From Custis we learn that "General Washington, in the prime of life, stood six feet two inches, and measured precisely six feet when attired for the grave." Custis also recorded that "Washington's powers were chiefly in his limbs: they were long, large and sinewy.... His frame showed an extraordinary development of bone and muscle; his joints were large, as were his feet; and could a cast have been preserved of his hand, to be exhibited in these degenerate days, it would be said to have belonged to the being of a fabulous age."

To illustrate his point, Custis then added this charming anecdote: "During Lafayette's visit to Mount Vernon in 1825, he said to the writer, 'I never saw so large a hand on any human being, as the general's. It was on this portico, in 1784, that you were introduced to me by the general. You were a very little gentleman, with a feather in your hat, and holding fast to *one finger* of the good general's remarkable hand, which was all that you could do, my dear sir, at that time.'"

So much for prelude. Now to record the facts that have served as a basis for the Potomac dollar-throwing episode.

On Page 482 of Custis' recollections this paragraph appears: "The power of Washington's arm was displayed in several memorable instances; in his throwing a stone from the bed of the stream to the top of Natural Bridge; another over the Palisades into the Hudson, and yet another across the Rappahannock, at Fredericksburg." Then, in order to set the matter straight for all time, Custis added the following: "Of the article with which he spanned this bold and navigable stream, there are various accounts. We are assured that it was a piece of slate, fashioned to about the size and shape of a dollar, and which, sent by an arm so strong, not only spanned the river, but took the ground at least thirty yards on the other side."

That should kill the story once and for all, but to show that myths take a long time to die, I'd like to end with two witty anecdotes bearing on the subject.

On November 19, 1951, when President Truman was addressing the National Cartoonist Association, he debunked the legend of Washington's throwing a dollar across the Potomac. Waxing specific, Truman said, "It was a Spanish piece of eight, and it was thrown across the Rappahannock. Any 10-year-old boy could throw a dime across at that place. But I am doubtful that Washington, with his acquisitive habits, would ever let loose of a Spanish piece of eight."

There is an even funnier yarn concerning the legendary episode.

Alice Roosevelt, before her marriage in 1906 to Nicholas Longworth, a longtime member of the U.S. House of Representatives, took a party of Englishmen on a visit to Mount Vernon. Pausing at a spot by the river, she remarked, "At this point Washington threw a dollar across the Potomac."

That didn't seem to impress the Britishers, one of whom commented tiredly, "Well, a dollar went further in those days, I believe."

"Yes, but Washington did more than that," the quick-witted Alice countered wickedly. "Once he chucked a sovereign across the Atlantic."

Hummingbird Stung the Brits

Although the details of the American victory over the British at Craney Island on June 22, 1813, which saved Norfolk and Portsmouth from being captured and pillaged, are fairly well known, there is another story dating from the same period involving a black man named Jasper and a British naval officer that deserves to be remembered.

To briefly recapitulate the background of the Norfolk area participation in the War of 1812, in February 1813 a formidable British squadron sailed through the Virginia Capes to blockade the Chesapeake Bay. This action bottled up the frigate Constellation in Norfolk harbor. But this was a blessing in disguise as the officers, sailors, marines and small boats of the frigate subsequently proved invaluable in defending the Norfolk area from the blockaders.

With the arrival of the British in Hampton Roads, hurried preparations for the defense of the area were coordinated under the direction of General Robert Barraud Taylor. Fortifications on the outskirts of Norfolk and Portsmouth were hastily thrown up, but Taylor had no idea of letting the enemy get that close to home if he could help it.

Commandeering every available vessel, Taylor threw a floating barrier across the mouth of the Elizabeth River, while Craney Island was strengthened with a fort and redoubts. Meanwhile, the already impressive British fleet was strengthened by new arrivals, after which the squadron sailed up to the mouth of the Nansemond River in full confidence of making short work of the defenses at Craney Island.

To ensure the fidelity of his men, the British admiral in charge of the expedition assured them that after Craney Island had fallen nothing would stand between them and Norfolk and Portsmouth. Once these were taken, he agreed to grant the attackers three days of unrestricted pillage and an additional reward of 20 pounds sterling. As an added inducement, they also were told that the loveliest ladies of the Norfolk area would be then at their disposal.

But this was not to be, for the British were so roundly defeated at Craney Island that they shifted their activities shortly afterward to the upper reaches of the Chesapeake Bay.

So much for the bleached bones of history. The story of the patriot named Jasper, who had his own way of discomfiting the enemy, is much more colorful.

While the British warships were anchored in Hampton Roads, Jasper made a little money by furnishing those on board with fresh vegetables and drinking water. On one occasion he was asked by an English naval officer if there were any hummingbirds in the area. When Jasper replied, "A plenty," he was commissioned to furnish the ornithological-minded Britisher with a few specimens, for which he was promised payment.

On the day specified for delivery, Jasper rowed out to the vessel, bringing along a sealed box. When this was delivered, he advised the officer to take it to his cabin, darken the room and prepare a quantity of sweetened water for the birds. He also cautioned that some time should be allowed to elapse before the box was opened as the hummingbirds were so fond of him they might follow him if they were freed too quickly. He was then paid and rowed for the shore.

The arrival of the hummingbirds created such interest that the officer and his friends lost no time in opening the box once it had been removed to his cabin. When that was done, it was found to contain two wasp nests, out of which the angry insects immediately swarmed and began making war on the enemy.

This caused a great hue and cry, and for a time it seemed as though the rapidly retreating Jasper would be killed by musket balls fired by the outraged Britons in his direction. Fortunately, he was not only a skilled oarsman but a good ducker, and he was soon out of range. From then on, he was known throughout the Norfolk area as "Hummingbird Jasper."

The Father of Grog

Although it might seem farfetched to couple George Washington's beloved Mount Vernon with the grog ration served aboard British naval vessels since the 1740s, the two have a proven connection that presumably could have been known to the Father of Our Country.

Mount Vernon was named by Lawrence Washington (1718-52), the older half-brother of the Father of His Country, for the British admiral, Edward Vernon (1684-1757), the Father of Grog. Lawrence Washington served under Vernon as a captain in the Virginia Militia in the joint army and naval attack on Spain's South American colonies during the New World phase of the War of the Austrian Succession. The relatively unknown fact, however, is that it was Admiral Vernon who issued the order instituting the grog tradition in the British Navy during that campaign.

Originally called Hunting Creek Plantation, the 5,000-acre tract, part of which later became Mount Vernon, was granted in 1674 to Nicholas Spencer and John Washington, the great-grandfather of Lawrence and George Washington.

The tract was divided in 1690 and the Washington holding became the property of Augustine Washington, Lawrence and George Washington's father, in 1726. Fourteen years later, Augustine Washington deeded Hunting Creek Plantation to Lawrence Washington, who had just come of age, and it was he who built the nucleus of the present Mount Vernon mansion and gave his home overlooking the Potomac its present name.

Meanwhile, war had broken out in 1740 between Great Britain and Spain, and Lawrence Washington volunteered for service in the Caribbean under Sir William Gooch, then lieutenant governor of Virginia. Setting out from Annapolis, Md., the Virginia troops soon became a part of a large-scale naval and army onslaught on Spain's South American ports headed by Admiral

Vernon.

At first successful, the expedition finally floundered at the disastrous siege of Cartagena, Colombia. Bickering among British army and naval commanders, combined with a lethal epidemic of tropical fever, finally forced Vernon to abandon the siege.

In the meantime, Governor Gooch, one of Virginia's most popular 18th century officials, had been seriously wounded when a 24-pound cannonball passed between his ankles, injuring both legs, while Lawrence Washington became so ill with fever he was forced to resign his commission and return to Virginia. His untimely death in 1752 was a great blow to his younger half-brother, George, who eventually acquired Lawrence Washington's property. Before his death, however, Lawrence Washington changed the name of Hunting Creek Plantation to Mount Vernon in honor of the British admiral. Since then, Mount Vernon and the name of Washington have been synonymous.

Now for the grog part of the story.

Until Admiral Vernon's order limiting the daily intake of alcohol, which was put into effect while Lawrence Washington served under him, every noncommissioned man in the British Navy was entitled to a daily ration of a pint of straight rum. Feeling that this was addling to his sailors' brains, particularly while they were operating in a tropical climate, Vernon launched a private war on drunkenness. In 1740, he decreed that all sailors under his command be forced to take their daily pint of rum diluted with a quart of water.

The order mandated by Vernon, who was not particularly popular with his officers or his men, caused a furor at first and the new drink was disparagingly referred to as "grog" by the admiral's disgruntled crews. In christening the drink "grog" the sailors were referring to one of the admiral's peculiarities, the wearing of a cloak of grogram, a coarse fabric of silk, worsted and mohair, often stiffened with gum to repel rain. This cloak, which was not a part of the regulation uniform of the British admirals of that time, had earned Vernon the opprobrious nickname of "Old Grogram," an appellation that eventually was truncated to "Old Grog."

Vernon's newly decreed nautical potation was therefore soon called "grog," the name it has continued to be known by. The sailors under Vernon eventually got used to the new drink, since it was better than no alcohol at all. And some of them found that by consuming the combined rum and water ration quickly they got as drunk as they had by swigging their ration of neat rum over a longer period. But over all, drunkenness in Vernon's command subsided.

Once Vernon's experiment had been tested and proved successful, other British admirals instituted similar regulations. The result was that "grog" took the place of neat rum as a daily dram in the British Navy, a tradition that holds today. The drink also added an adjective to the English language for by 1770, "groggy" was being used in daily speech to denote the condition of one who had imbibed too freely.

As for the alcoholic tradition in the American Navy, it followed the British custom until World War I, when Josephus Daniels, then secretary of the Navy, banished alcohol for drinking purposes from all American naval vessels.

Daniels' order has recently been somewhat modified, however, for today some Navy ships are permitted to carry a small supply of alcoholic beverages to be used only on shore for entertainment purposes. Also, any crewman is permitted two cans of beer if his ship has been continuously at sea for 144 days.

To return to Daniels' World War I prohibitive order, it was naturally unpopular with habitual boozers, one of whom blasted the Tar Heel naval secretary with the following doggerel:

When I was a lad I pondered some
On the horrible effects of the Demon Rum;
I scorned to dally with the dread highball
And I never saw a bottle of champagne at all.
I kept away from guzzling men
And now I am the ruler of the U.S.N.

Stamped With Faith

Virginia-born William Short (1759-1849), who went along as secretary of the American legation when Thomas Jefferson was appointed minister to France in 1784 and who subsequently filled many important American diplomatic posts in Europe, is an almost forgotten figure in the early history of the republic.

Even so, Short's lifelong association with the Sage of Monticello, of whom he was a favorite protege, resulted in an intimate correspondence between the two men.

Short's letters to Jefferson are apparently no longer extant, but 145 letters Jefferson wrote to Short, concerning everything from politics to the purchase of a Neapolitan macaroni-making machine, are now among the treasures of Swem Memorial Library of the College of William and Mary in Williamsburg.

How they were acquired is a fascinating story. But before I give the details, it might be a good idea to review Short's career, as aspects of it had an important bearing on how and why William and Mary was chosen as the repository of his carefully hoarded collection of Jefferson's letters.

Born at Spring Garden plantation in Surry County, Short was a son of William Short, a wealthy planter, and Elizabeth Skipwith Short, a daughter of Sir Peyton Skipwith, one of the few members of the British landed gentry who emigrated to Virginia before the Revolutionary War.

Educated at the College of William and Mary, Short was an original member of the Phi Beta Kappa fraternity and was its president from 1778 until its temporary suspension at the college in 1781.

After serving as Jefferson's secretary in Paris, Short was made *charge d'affaires,* his commission being the first one signed by George Washington as president.

Having been absent from the United States in the

diplomatic service for 16 years, Short returned to this country in 1801. Two years later, he had his portrait painted by Rembrandt Peale, with a background depicting the Greek ruins of Paestum in southern Italy, where Short, as an admirer of all things classical, had visited during his European years. The portrait is now in the Joseph and Margaret Muscarelle Museum of Art at William and Mary.

In 1849, Short was active in the revival of the Phi Beta Kappa chapter at William and Mary, and on December 5 that year he died at age 90 in Philadelphia, having never married.

So much for Short. Enter Dr. Earl Gregg Swem (1870-1965), librarian of William and Mary from 1920 to 1944, for whom Swem Library was named. He is the principal in the story of how Short's Jefferson letters wound up in the archives of his alma mater.

As Swem used to recall the incident, one steaming summer day, shortly after he took over the library, he received an urgent telephone call from Dr. J.A.C. Chandler, president of the college, asking him to call on him immediately. Pulling on a coat reluctantly, Swem walked over to the president's house.

There he found two elderly ladies clothed in deep mourning. Both identified themselves as collateral descendants of Short. Having driven all the way from Tennessee, they wanted Swem to accompany them the next day to Spring Garden, across the James River so they could visit their ancestors' tombs.

"I consented, of course, although I didn't have the faintest idea of the location of the tombs," Swem said later. "Then one of the ladies opened her pocketbook and handed me Short's original Phi Beta Kappa key. I'll tell you, I was visibly shaken!"

The key, incidentally, is now a treasured possession of the College of William and Mary.

Swem accompanied the two ladies the next day to Surry County, where they eventually located the Short burying ground. And even though one of the ladies nearly suffered a broken leg when she stepped into a deep hole, they were pleased with Swem's courtesy. Thanking him, they returned to Tennessee, and Swem considered the episode finished.

But he was wrong, for the biblical adage concerning casting one's bread upon the waters, in which Swem was a great believer, paid off with dividends a short time later.

One year after the tomb-visiting episode, Swem received a letter from one of the ladies, expressing such pleasure in what he had done for her that she had decided to present the college library with 145 original letters Jefferson had written to Short and which she had inherited.

"Earl didn't sleep for a week," his wife used to interrupt at that point of his narrative.

"Well, be that as it may," Swem would continue, "the letters finally arrived. One end of the parcel was ripped out, and the wrapping was so careless that it was a God's wonder the thing ever got through the mails."

Then, after a significant pause, during which his humorous old eyes would twinkle brightly behind his thick glasses, Swem would add, "Think of it — 145 irreplaceable, original letters of Thomas Jefferson, worth millions of dollars, sent through the mails in a loosely tied bundle!"

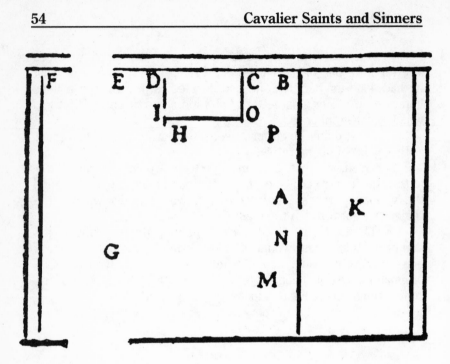

The first American murder diagram (1766)

'X' Marks ye Spot

The first American newspaper murder diagram, a crude woodcut that enabled titillated Virginians to follow the actions leading up to a brutal slaying, was printed in Purdie & Dixon's Virginia Gazette in Williamsburg on July 18, 1766.

The principals were Robert Routledge, a Scottish merchant, and Colonel John Chiswell, a hot-tempered Virginia aristocrat who fatally stabbed Routledge in a tavern brawl. Not only was the case the most sensational crime committed in the Old Dominion during the 18th century, it caused an uproar among the middle-class Virginians who believed Chiswell received preferential treatment from his upper-crust friends who tried to excuse his rash action.

Routledge, who lived south of the Appomattox River in Prince Edward County, had come to Virginia around 1746. Known as "a worthy man, of strict honesty and sincerity, a man incapable of fraud and hypocrisy," he was regarded as one of the most substantial traders in the colony. Chiswell, Routledge's murderer, was a Virginia grandee. Married to Elizabeth Randolph, a daughter of Colonel William Randolph II of Chatsworth, a connection that linked him with most of the first families of Virginia, Chiswell cut a wide swath in the Old Dominion of his time. Although energetic and enterprising, the colonel had a very serious character flaw — a hair-trigger temper. When he imagined he had suffered an indignity from anyone belonging to the lower orders, he reacted impulsively without any thought for the consequences.

The murder took place on June 3, 1766, in Benjamin Mosby's tavern at Cumberland Court House where Routledge and a group of cronies had been carousing for the better part of the day. Toward nightfall, Chiswell arrived at the tavern and began to talk, according to the newspaper accounts, "in an important manner," punctuating his rant with "illiberal oaths." Routledge, who was by then completely drunk, took exception to Chiswell's remarks, at which the colonel blazed out at the Scotsman, calling him, among other things a "Presbyterian fellow" as well as "a fugitive rebel, a villain who came to Virginia to cheat and defraud men of property."

In branding Routledge "a fugitive rebel," Chiswell intentionally linked him to the abortive Scottish rebellion of 1745, in which Charles Edward Stuart, sentimentally remembered as "Bonnie Prince Charley," unsuccessfully attempted to regain the British throne from the Hanoverian dynasty. As far as is known, however, Routledge had no Jacobite sympathies. Chiswell's reference to Routledge as a "Presbyterian" was also intended as a slur, since anyone then belonging to that sect was regarded as an apostate in Virginia where the Established Church reigned supreme. Finally, in calling Routledge a "fellow," Chiswell implied that he was base-born, and therefore not a gentleman.

In the Virginia of that day, these epithets were fighting words, and it is not surprising that Routledge reacted by flinging a glass of wine in the colonel's face. Chiswell attempted to heave a bowl of "bumbo," a potent punch made of rum or gin, sugar, water and nutmeg, at Routledge but was restrained by the other topers. He then attacked the Scotsman with a candlestick and a pair of fire tongs.

Routledge's friends again intervened, whereupon Chiswell, who was perfectly sober, ordered his servant to bring him his sword from the adjoining room, threatening to kill him if he did not comply, all of which brings us to America's first printed murder diagram. By consulting the letters shown in the woodcut at the end of this chapter, it is easy to follow what happened from then on.

Chiswell received his sword from his servant in the adjoining room (K). Re-entering the public room (G), he took up his station in front of the fireplace (M). When the company saw his naked sword they tried to persuade him to desist, but he moved close to the wall (N), swearing "that he would run any man through the body who would attempt to take his sword.... Then he ordered in an imperious tone that Routledge should depart out of the room, as unworthy to appear in such company, and swore that if he did not immediately get out, he would kill him."

Routledge insisted upon remaining, saying he had no grudge against Chiswell, but as he was completely intoxicated, a friend eased him toward a rear door (E-F). Meanwhile, Chiswell, continuing to abuse Routledge, moved along the wall (A to B), at which point the distance between the Scotsman and himself was 6 feet (B-E), with a table (C-D) standing between them and the wall. In order to retain his sword, Chiswell tried to get behind the table, and while Routledge stood by the back door (E), the colonel again called him a "Presbyterian fellow."

Enraged, Routledge staggered forward (I), saying, "He thought himself as good a fellow as John Chiswell." At that remark, the colonel shifted to (P), later advancing to (O), then lunged, stabbing Routledge (I) through the heart, killing him instantly. At the same time, Chiswell's sword passed through the coat of another man (H), who was standing near Routledge. Also, at the time of the fatal thrust, someone grabbed Chiswell from behind, but he calmly remarked it was too late, adding: "He is dead, and I killed him."

Then, turning to his servant, the colonel directed him to take his sword and "clean it carefully and rub it over with tallow, lest it should rust," after which he faced the horrified spectators and remarked, "He deserved his fate, damn him, I aimed at his heart and I have hit it." He then "called for a bowl of toddy, and drank very freely," so that by the time the sheriff arrived "he was somewhat intoxicated."

Despite his high social standing, Chiswell was arrested and lodged in the county jail. A few days later he was charged with "feloniously murdering Robert Routledge" and was sent on to Williamsburg in the custody of an under-sheriff to stand trial at the next session of the General Court. Meanwhile, the news spread rapidly through the plantation society to which Chiswell belonged, causing the colonel's highly placed friends to act on his behalf. Since the General Court was not in session, three of its members intercepted the murderer and his guard before they reached Williamsburg and admitted Chiswell to bail "out of season," a highhanded act that threw "the whole country in a ferment." Consequently, not only the Virginia Gazette published detailed accounts of the murder, but reports of the crime appeared in other newspapers throughout the colonies, as well as in London.

In the meantime, fearing mob violence as the result of angry feelings held against him among the middle and lower classes of Virginia, Chiswell committed suicide on October 15, 1766, by hanging himself in his Williamsburg home rather than stand trial, be judged guilty, and be executed as a felon.

Even then the consensus was that the colonel had been spirited out of the colony by his influential friends and that his coffin was either empty or contained the corpse of another man.

When Chiswell's remains were brought to Scotchtown, his country seat in Hanover County, for interment, the immense crowd that had gathered there would not permit burial to take place until the body was identified beyond question. That task was performed by Colonel William Dabney, an intimate friend of Chiswell's, who had the trust of the exasperated people who feared that trickery on the part of the colonel's highly placed friends had enabled him to escape.

Here Lies Jefferson

Anyone who comes away from a visit to Monticello thinking he has seen the original monument of Thomas Jefferson in the family graveyard there has another think coming, to use a time-honored satirical Virginia folk saying.

The granite obelisk-shaped monument now marking Jefferson's last resting place, a replica twice the size of the original cenotaph, was authorized by Congress in 1878 and was placed in its present position over Jefferson's remains in 1883.

Jefferson's original monument, which had been badly vandalized by souvenir hunters, was then presented by his descendants to the University of Missouri, where, apart from the actual funerary inscription which is carved on a separate slab of white marble, it is now proudly displayed on the university campus at Columbia, Mo.

Jefferson, who was born on April 13, 1743, died on July 4, 1826. Shortly afterward his descendants discovered among his papers a rough sketch of a tombstone he had designed for himself. To summarize his wishes, the Sage of Monticello informed his heirs that he would be gratified if they would provide a "plain die or cube...surmounted by an Obelisk" to mark his grave.

Eschewing the fulsome epitaphs which were then fashionable, Jefferson went on to desire that only the following be engraved on his monument: "Here was buried/**THOMAS JEFFERSON**/Author of the Declaration of Independence/of the Statute of Virginia for religious freedom and/Father of the University of Virginia."

Jefferson's estate was so encumbered with debt at the time of his death that his favorite grandson and executor, Thomas Jefferson Randolph, was unable to immediately carry out his grandfather's instructions. Meanwhile, Monticello was sold to pay off Jefferson's debts, but the family graveyard was reserved for the use of Jefferson's heirs, who finally erected the monument around 1833.

One of the earliest owners of Monticello was Navy Lieutenant Uriah Levy, an ardent Jefferson admirer from New York. He attempted to keep up the badly deteriorating mansion and to fend off vandals from the Jefferson family cemetery.

Although it has no connection with Jefferson's monument, there is an interesting anecdote concerning the years of Levy's tenancy. When Levy bought Monticello, he fell heir to one of the oldest Jefferson family servants. After the later's new master returned from abroad, extensive improvements were made to the grounds, and the old caretaker had occasion one day to show some visitors around the garden. Calling their attention with some pride and more embarrassment to the nude statues of Venus and Ceres, he exclaimed, "Them ladies is Mis' Venus an' her daughter. Mr. Levy knowed 'em in Paris."

Levy died in 1862. He willed Monticello to either the state of Virginia or the U.S. government, providing that whichever accepted his gift would keep up the estate. The will was contested by Levy's heirs, however, and eventually Monticello was acquired by Levy's nephew, Jefferson Monroe Levy. Under his ownership Monticello went to the dogs, and the Jefferson graveyard was shamefully desecrated. During the same period an erroneous rumor circulated nationally claiming that Jefferson's original monument had been destroyed.

This caused his descendants, some public officials, members of the press and a few concerned private individuals to attempt to raise funds to erect another monument in place of the original one that, contrary to rumor, was still intact but badly battered.

Their efforts were rewarded in 1878 when Congress appropriated $5,000 to erect another and larger monument using Jefferson's original design as a model. Four years later, Congress raised the appropriation to $10,000 to cover the cost of the new shaft and to repair the graveyard at Monticello. While this was being done, Jefferson's descendants received numerous requests from patriotic societies as well as several public and educational institutions offering to give the original monument a place of safekeeping.

Eventually the University of Missouri was awarded the coveted granite shaft. This was because of "Jefferson's lifelong labors in behalf of state-supported education (Jefferson, in effect, originated the concept of the state university, and Missouri's university had projected a curriculum and a concept of higher education similar to those Jefferson had put into practice some years before at the University of Virginia), and because of his faith in the western portions of the nation."

The transfer of what was left of the original monument from Monticello to Missouri was entrusted to Alexander Frederick Fleet, a native of Virginia who was then professor of Greek at the University of Missouri. Fleet supervised the re-erection of the monument near the university's Academic Hall, after which an elaborate thank-you letter honoring the occasion was printed on white satin and sent to the Jefferson descendants who had authorized the transfer.

Until 1892, the original Jefferson monument remained near the Academic Hall. But that burned and the original marble plaque with Jefferson's inscription, attached to the obelisk, was "cracked and burned." So the shaft was moved to a safer place.

Taking no chances that the precious marble plaque listing Jefferson's outstanding public contributions would again be damaged, the university faculty ordered that it be repaired and stored in a vault at the University of Missouri. Since then, it has remained under lock and key except for one day during the year, Jefferson's birthday on April 13, when it is proudly exhibited in honor of the man who is sometimes called the Apostle of Democracy.

James Lafayette, Patriot Spy

James, a black man owned by William Armistead of New Kent County, did as much, and possibly more, to bring about the surrender of Cornwallis at Yorktown on October 19, 1781, than many of the white American officers and soldiers from whom present-day Sons and Daughters of the American Revolution proudly claim their descent.

Born in 1748, James was 33 at the time Cornwallis' army invaded Virginia from the Carolinas in 1781. Occupying Richmond and Williamsburg first, the British later moved on to Portsmouth, from which they were transported by ships to Yorktown. At that time the Continental forces in Virginia were commanded by the Marquis de Lafayette, and it was particularly fortunate for the American cause that William Armistead, James' master, was a commissary responsible for provisioning Lafayette's troops.

Realizing the importance of securing military information from the British, Lafayette planted a spy in Cornwallis' household to garner such data, but getting it through the lines posed a difficult problem. At that juncture, James, who was noted for his shrewdness and intelligence, rose to the occasion. Trusting that the successful risking of his neck as a secret agent might eventually gain him his freedom, he requested his master to permit him to volunteer as a spy for Lafayette, a petition Armistead readily granted.

Acting as a forager, in which capacity he was able to move easily through the British lines to collect food from the surrounding country for the tables at British headquarters, James not only conveyed invaluable information concerning Cornwallis' plans to Lafayette from the American spy already working in the British general's headquarters, but he also carried written instructions to other spies and letters "from the Marquiss into the Enemies lines, of the most secret and important kind; the possession of which if discovered on him would have most certainly have endangered (his) life."

Having in some now unknown manner attracted the attention of Cornwallis and his staff, James took the precaution of allaying their suspicions by volunteering to spy on Lafayette's actions. This not only improved his own cover but also enabled him to discern the enemy's intentions more accurately based on the type of information Cornwallis wanted him to collect on Lafayette's movements. As a result, from August 1781 until Cornwallis' surrender two months later, James became a familiar figure around the British headquarters at Yorktown. During that time he provided Cornwallis with sufficient information to keep him satisfied but not enough to bring harm to Lafayette's forces. Meanwhile, he continued to smuggle military secrets out of the British camp, and thereby "kept open a channel of the most useful communications to the army of the state."

One of James' exploits has been preserved in detail. Once when Cornwallis appeared on the verge of making good his threat of capturing Lafayette, a ruse conceived by the marquis and carried out by James staved off the superior British force.

Lafayette gave James a piece of paper carelessly torn in half, ostensibly an order to General Daniel Morgan to take up his station in support of Lafayette's right flank. When James appeared at Cornwallis' headquarters with the two pieces of paper, the British general asked to examine them. Obliging, James explained they were only a couple of scraps he had picked up and brought along not knowing what they said, since he could not read.

Piecing them together, Cornwallis was astonished to learn of General Morgan's arrival in support of Lafayette when the American general was supposed to be several days' march away. The ruse worked as Lafayette hoped it would and Cornwallis did not attack.

Still another anecdote concerning James had an amusing climax. Two days after Cornwallis surrendered, Lafayette was told that the British general was anxious to meet him. The next day the marquis visited Cornwallis, at which time they reviewed the tactics of the Yorktown campaign, after which Lafayette invited Cornwallis to dine with him the next day. While they were eating, James, the double spy, walked into the room and the British general suddenly realized how Lafayette had been able to anticipate and outmaneuver his movements successfully.

With the coming of peace, James' spying activities ceased, but before Lafayette departed for France he presented him with a letter of commendation, that read:

"This is to certify that the Bearer by the name of James has done Essential Services to me while I had the Honour to Command in this State. His intelligences from the Enemy's Camp were industriously collected and most faithfully deliver'd. He properly acquitted himself with some important Commissions I gave him and appears to me entitled to every reward his Situation can admit of. Done under my hand, Richmond, November 21st, 1784.

"LaFayette."

James had to wait two years for his reward, but on January 9, 1786, with the consent of his master, he was declared a free man by a special act of the Virginia legislature, at which time he chose Armistead as his middle name and adopted the surname of Lafayette in honor of the French general he had served so faithfully. Taking up his residence with his wife and son in New Kent County, the former slave, who from then on proudly called himself James Armistead Lafayette, eventually owned three slaves, a not unusual situation for Virginia free blacks at that time.

In 1818, when he was 70, he applied to the legislature for help during his declining years. The petition was approved and the former slave, who had meanwhile taught himself to sign his name, was allowed $60 for his "present relief" and a $40 annual pension for his Revolutionary services. But that was not James Armistead Lafayette's final reward.

In 1824, when Lafayette visited the United States for the last time, he made a pilgrimage to Yorktown. Because of the crowds surrounding his carriage, Lafayette's progress was slow. Then, suddenly, in the midst of the enthusiastic throng, Lafayette recognized 76-year-old James Armistead Lafayette, the black man whose skillful espionage had contributed largely toward the French and American victory 43 years earlier. In reporting the event, the Richmond Enquirer said: "A black man even, who had rendered him services by way of information as a spy, for which he had been liberated by the state, was recognized by him (Lafayette) in the crowd, called to him by name, and taken into his embraces."

Four years later, James Armistead Lafayette gained additional fame when James Heath, a Virginia author, made him a subsidiary hero in a novel called *Edge Hill,* using Revolutionary Virginia as its background. Increasing recognition also prompted John Blennerhasset Martin, a Richmond artist, to ask James Armistead Lafayette to sit for his portrait. The picture, now owned by the Valentine Museum in Richmond, depicts a proud and handsome old man with shrewd eyes and a humorous mouth, attired in a blue coat accented with eagle-decorated brass buttons.

Six years after his memorable reunion with Lafayette at Yorktown, James Armistead Lafayette died in New Kent County on August 9, 1830, at the age of 82. He was a true Virginia patriot of the American War for Independence.

Part 3: Brave Men, Bold Women

Pluck in Petticoats

To hear most genealogical-minded Virginians talk you'd think their earliest colonial ancestresses all belonged to the prissier variety of females. But those were few and far between even during the morally-corseted Victorian era when it was considered ladylike to affect la-de-da airs.

Frontier conditions (and it is well to remember that early Virginia was a large segment of the Wild West of its time) are never conducive to artificial gentility and refinement. As a consequence, it was a matter of expediency for a spirited woman to assert herself in a male-dominated world. This resulted in many colonial dames of the Old Dominion being much more aggressive than their descendants like to picture them.

Surviving records prove conclusively that the assertions of the moonlight and magnolia school of Virginia ancestor worshipers who insist that their female forebears were "Southern ladies of the old school" are figments of overly romantic imaginations. It took more than refined and exaggerated sensibilities to survive during the early days of the Old Dominion. The ability to shoot a gun or risk male displeasure by asserting one's rights was far more important to many robust pioneer women than flirting with a fan.

Take the case of Mistress Alice Proctor, who braved the Atlantic in 1621 to join her husband, who had settled much earlier on the James River. When the first Indian massacre broke like a bloody wave over the Tidewater region in 1622, Mistress Proctor was alone on her frontier post. Although she is referred to in the old records as "a proper, civil, modest Gentlewoman," her social standing did not keep her from grabbing the first gun handy and giving the Indians such a hot reception that they beat a hasty retreat.

Dame Alice Clawson, who lived on the Eastern Shore of Virginia during the middle years of the 17th century, was another forthright character. Her wayward husband returned after an overlong period with the Nanticoke Indians and refused to give up the redskin concubine he had brazenly brought home with him. His no-nonsense wife haled him before the justices and pleaded her case so eloquently that she wound up being the first Virginia woman to obtain a permanent legal separation from a two-timing spouse.

Then there was Mrs. Frances Jones, the ancestress of many prominent Southside Virginia families, who lived near the North Carolina border. An account of her strong-armed activities is included in the Boundary Line Proceedings of 1710, where the commissioners noted: "It is said of Mrs. Jones that she is a very civil woman and shews nothing of Immodesty in her carriage, yet she will carry a gun in the woods and kill deer, turkeys, &c., shoot down wild cattle, catch and tye hoggs, knock down beeves with an ax and perform the most manful Exercises as well as most men in those parts."

Unwed mothers and out-of-wedlock pregnancies were only too prevalent during Virginia's first century. Surviving court records contain considerable spice concerning the female transgressors and the Lotharios who got them into trouble. As a rule the guilty parties philosophically accepted the punishments handed down by the justices but there was one female black sheep who proved to be a damsel of spirit.

In September 1642, Edith Tooker of Lower Norfolk County was convicted of having a child out of wedlock and was ordered to do penance in the parish church the following Sunday at the time of divine service wearing nothing but a white sheet to cover her nakedness. Edith was further instructed to stand on a stool in full view of the congregation and to publicly acknowledge her fall from grace.

After being led into the church and mounting the stool, the culprit was urged by the minister to repent the "foul sin" she had committed. But Edith Tooker was a woman of mettle. Turning a deaf ear to the parson's prosings, she "did like a most obstinate and graceless person, cut and mangle the sheet wherein she did penance." For those shenanigans, Edith was condemned to receive 20 lashes and was further commanded to appear again in a white sheet in the same church on "the following Sabbath fortnight."

Colonial Virginia also had at least one recorded instance of an independent woman who turned the tables on the traditional male-dominated role as far as marriage proposals were concerned.

Betsy Hansford of York County, the heroine of the story, was much cleverer than the more widely publicized Priscilla Mullens of Plymouth, Mass., whose unimaginative "Why don't you speak for yourself, John?" speech got her the husband of her choice. Betsy went Priscilla one better and snared her man, a minister of the gospel, with a quotation from Holy Writ, with which he should have been familiar but apparently was not.

In 1769, when one of Betsy's rejected suitors begged the Reverend John Camm, then president of the College of William and Mary, to plead his suit for him, Betsy's future husband paid her a visit and pleaded the young man's case. When Betsy remained adamant, Camm quoted several pertinent passages from the Bible to drive home his point. Still, Betsy would not budge. Finally, after the parson had exhausted his texts, Betsy told him to go home and look into the Scriptures at 2 Samuel 12:7, and he would find the reason for her refusal. Camm hurried home to look up the passage. There, in bold type, he read: "And Nathan said to David: Thou art the Man." It goes without saying that Betsy and Camm were married shortly afterward.

This is amusing enough, but in the final analysis it was Sarah Harrison Blair, the first Virginia feminist, who refused to comply with the technicalities of the marriage ceremony, and thereby qualified as the most unusual Virginia colonial dame of her time. One glance at her waspish portrait, painted after her marriage to the Reverend James Blair, commissary of the Bishop of London and the founder and first president of the College of William and Mary, is enough to convince even the most confirmed romantic that she was fully capable of any of the capriciousness that contemporary gossip attributes to her.

Born in 1670 at Wakefield, the home of her father, Benjamin Harrison, in Surry County, Sarah kept a low profile until 1687 when she put her signature to an agreement "cordially promising" not to marry anyone else but a certain William Roscow as long as he was alive. Two months later, however, she repudiated this agreement and married the Reverend James Blair. A contemporary account of the wedding not only reveals that it was performed with difficulty, but also shows that Sarah was the outspoken Virginia militant feminist of her day.

The old record says: "When Mr. James Blair was married to Mrs. Sarah Harrison, it was done by one Mr. Smith, when she was to say, Obey, She said No obey, upon which He refused to proceed & the second time she said No Obey & then he refused again to proceed. The third time she said No Obey, yet the sd Mr. Smith went on with the rest of the ceremony."

Sarah's obstinacy was only a prelude to what was to follow, for during the remainder of her life she became a petticoat power in colonial Virginia politics.

Toward the end, however, according to an entry in the diary of Colonel William Byrd II of Westover, she relaxed the reins because of an over-fondness for drink. The urbane colonel had been in Williamsburg on business. Dropping by the commissary's house on his way home, he discovered Mrs. Blair in a deplorable state for a clergyman's wife.

In a titillating entry in his diary dated March 2, 1709, Byrd wrote: "I was very much surprised to find Mrs. Blair drunk, which is growing pretty common with her, and her relatives disguise it under the name of consolation."

Four years later, Sarah Blair died and was buried in the churchyard at Jamestown, but the old records have kept her memory as green as the blown glass bottles that contained her favorite potations.

Gabriel's Slave Revolt

The failure of Gabriel's Insurrection, the most ominous slave conspiracy in Virginia's history, which was halted by betrayal and spectacular natural phenomena in August 1800, was a classic example of Robert Burns' famous poetical adage: "The best laid schemes of mice and men gang aft a-gley."

Gabriel's Insurrection, one of approximately 250 revolts and conspiracies in the history of American slavery, was detected before it got out of hand. In the entire history of slavery in North America only three full-scale slave insurrections matured to the point that whites and blacks fought pitched battles. These were the Stono Slave Conspiracy of 1739, which took place in South Carolina; an uprising on several Louisiana plantations in 1811, and the more famous Nat Turner's Rebellion, which cut a bloody swath across Southampton County in 1831.

Even so, Gabriel's Insurrection, which is practically forgotten today, would have wreaked even greater death and destruction than the three other revolts combined had not blacks loyal to their masters betrayed its battle plans in the nick of time. Even the thought of what might have happened if the rebellion led by Gabriel Prosser in 1800 had succeeded is appalling, for thousands of slaves in the Richmond area and other localities throughout Virginia had obviously banded together with one objective in mind — the annihilation of the entire slave-owning population of the Tidewater area of the Old Dominion.

The genesis of the revolt went back to the Revolutionary War when many Virginia blacks fought in the Continental Army against Great Britain. Some of these patriots had been promised their freedom for their services, but few were emancipated once peace was declared. Then, a few years after Yorktown, rumors of the successful revolt of the slaves of Santo Domingo, in the West Indies, beginning in 1791, began to filter through to the United States.

In Virginia, this event was brought home forcibly when 137 square-rigged vessels loaded with Santo Domingo refugees sailed into Hampton Roads in 1793. Many of these refugees, including the well-known Bilisoly family of Portsmouth, settled in the Norfolk area, but many moved on to Richmond and other parts of the state.

Loyal slaves who had fled with their masters to Virginia were not long in imparting what had happened in the French colony to native-born Virginia blacks who had become increasingly bitter because the freedom that had been promised them for their Revolutionary service had been ignored or forgotten. This trickery presumably fueled the revolt that was ultimately led by Gabriel Prosser.

The same month the terrified refugees arrived in Virginia from Santo Domingo, a prominent white Richmond citizen informed Governor Henry ("Light Horse Harry") Lee that he had heard two black men conversing outside his bedroom window one night concerning a plot to "kill the white people...between this and the fifteenth of October," at which time the plotters specified that the same barbarous methods which had been used by the slaves in Santo Domingo would be used in Virginia.

Steps were immediately taken to guard against such an uprising, either in the Richmond or other Virginia areas, but the authorities in the next decade did not take into consideration the powerful black man known to his followers as "General Gabriel."

A 24-year-old trusted slave of Thomas H. Prosser of Brookfield plantation in Henrico County, Gabriel, with the aid of other persuasive conspirators, between 1799 and 1800 secretly planned the wholesale massacre of Richmond's slave-owning population, after which the insurrection was to continue in other parts of the state. Only two people of the class that the revolt meant to exterminate were to be spared. These were Governor James Monroe, who was to be held hostage, and Mrs. Mary Randolph, the celebrated Richmond hostess, who was to become Gabriel's cook because of her knowledge of the culinary arts.

Testimony taken after the failure of the insurrection indicated that most of the plans were made at religious gatherings, fish fries and barbecues, and in the kitchens of the conspirators' masters and mistresses. Also, in anticipation of the event, swords fashioned from scythes, pikes, spears, knives and crossbows were made by Gabriel's followers, who also stole and stockpiled muskets and gunpowder from their masters' homes and molded bullets. So lax were the precautions in Richmond that Gabriel, or one of his confederates, managed to gain access to the State Capitol on a Sunday, when it was supposedly closed, to take a mental inventory of what arms were stored there.

Since most of the conspirators lived in or near Richmond, the master plan concentrated on that city. If all had gone well, a small band of Gabriel's followers would have entered Richmond after midnight and set fire to the warehouses along the waterfront, reasoning that the white population would set out *en masse* to quench the flames. While this was being attempted, Gabriel and his armed band of around 1,000 slaves would enter the city, take over the public buildings and then massacre most of the citizenry.

Two things happened that wrecked Gabriel's well-laid plans. On Saturday, August 30, 1800, two black men, Pharaoh and Tom, went to their master, Mosby Sheppard, a leading Henrico County planter, and revealed that the plot was to be put into execution that night. Sheppard hurried immediately to Governor Monroe, who called out the militia. Meanwhile, Mother Nature stepped in, and that afternoon the Richmond area was visited by a tremendous thunderstorm with torrential rains that inundated the area for miles around. Nevertheless, Gabriel's faithful followers gatherer at the appointed time and place west of the city and would have marched on Richmond had not their leader, although oblivious of the fact that his plans had been betrayed, postponed the operation until the next night.

When that night came, Governor Monroe had so successfully alerted Richmond's population that the plan was abandoned, and Gabriel and his principal followers fled. Most of them were promptly captured, but Gabriel managed to elude the authorities until September 24, 1800.

After hiding in the swamps east of Richmond for some time, he hailed the *Mary*, a three-masted schooner headed down the James River on her way to Norfolk. Once aboard, he was immediately recognized by Isham and Billy, two slave members of the crew, who went to the captain, Richardson Taylor, and reported that the man he had picked up was none other than "General Gabriel."

An anti-slavery Methodist, Taylor refused to act, but when the vessel reached Norfolk, Billy, or one of his friends, sought out the town constables. Gabriel was taken into custody and returned to Richmond in irons. Refusing to talk to Governor Monroe or anyone else concerning the plot he had masterminded, he was tried and condemned to be hanged, along with around 35 other conspirators. Even so, that was a relatively small number, considering the thousands of discontented blacks throughout Virginia who were supposedly involved in the plot.

But the death of Gabriel and his co-conspirators did not quench the longing for freedom among Virginia's slaves, and 31 years later the state experienced a similar if less ambitious outbreak. That was Nat Turner's Insurrection in Southampton County in 1831, a conspiracy that made such an indelible impression on the entire nation that Gabriel's earlier aborted attempt is now only a minor footnote in Virginia's long history.

A Flight to Remember

American aeronautical history began in early 1793 when Jean Pierre Francois Blanchard (1753-1809) soared above the courtyard of the Walnut Street Prison in Philadelphia in the first successful balloon flight in the United States.

The takeoff was witnessed by thousands of excited spectators headed by George Washington, then serving his second term as president.

Blanchard, who had made 44 successful balloon ascents in various European countries, including the first aeronautical crossing of the English Channel from Dover to France in 1785, had arrived in Philadelphia from England aboard the ship *Ceres* on December 9, 1792. At that time he learned that several previous aeronautical experiments had been attempted in this country, the "ill success of which had disappointed the expectations of the subscribers."

Blanchard, a product of the Age of Enlightenment, was fortunate in choosing Philadelphia as the launching pad for his balloon, for the city was then not only the nation's second capital but the hub of scientific, artistic and intellectual activities in the New World. Washington furnished Blanchard with an explanatory letter to take on his first American balloon flight in case he might be regarded as a space alien when he landed. Other scientific-minded Americans including Thomas Jefferson were on hand when he headed skyward above the City of Brotherly Love.

Blanchard's flight was successful. He descended without incident 46 minutes after his takeoff near Woodbury, N.J., completing a 15-mile flight. Sympathetic observers helped load his deflated balloon on a wagon and escorted him back to Philadelphia in triumph.

His first act there was to call on Washington to thank him for his patronage. He gave the president the flag he had taken aloft with him, bearing the American ensign on one side and the

French tricolor on the other, as a souvenir of America's first successful balloon flight.

Later, Blanchard wrote an account of his flight titled *Journal of My Forty-Fifth Ascension, Being the First Performed in America on the Ninth of January, 1793,* which he dedicated to Washington, eulogizing him as "The Patron of Liberty, the Laws, and the Fine Arts."

Blanchard's ascension kicked off others throughout the United States, but most of these were unmanned flights. As far as is known, the first balloon exhibition in Norfolk took place on August 19, 1819, from the yard of Deford's Tavern and Bath House opposite the Fenchurch Street Theater.

The basket of this balloon, "about the size of a hogshead," was empty, but later, on August 30, 1819, a "Mr. Allen," the entrepreneur for the earlier flight, sent up a much larger balloon near Armistead's Rope Walk, the basket of which contained a cat.

In reporting the event, The Beacon for August 31, 1819, said: "The Balloon ascended in a very majestic style, and after it had progressed a few hundred yards, the Parachute separated the the **CAT** unhurt.... A large concourse of citizens assembled to witness the agreeable spectacle."

Even so, not all Norfolk balloon trips were so successful. For instance, late in July 1893, curiosity seekers flocked to Ocean View to witness a highly publicized aeronautical show staged by the Shannon Balloon Co., headed by "Professor" Harry Hutcheson, in which a 19-year-old woman named Ruth Hutcheson was scheduled to give the spectators something to talk about.

Unfortunately, the balloon in which Miss Hutcheson and her pug dog were passengers ran into difficulties a few moments after the takeoff, and she and her pet wound up being suspended from a rope attached to the balloon's basket about 120 feet above the heads of the horrified spectators. Losing her grip, she and the pug landed in the branches of a tall pine tree, from which she and her pet were rescued by a Norfolk painter named Foster.

Undaunted, Miss Hutcheson decided to try again the next day, and The Virginian announced "Miss Hutcheson will make another ascension tonight, but the sight of a pretty girl in black tights and red silk blouse 120 feet up a tree will not be repeated."

This statement probably seemed safe enough to the reporter who wrote the story, but what happened on the second attempt was not only unscheduled but even more exciting than the fiasco of the previous day.

In reporting what took place, The Virginian said: "Fully 1,000 people went down to Ocean View to witness the balloon flight and to see the tree from which the young woman was heroically rescued by Mr. Foster. Little did they expect in a short time to see a repetition of the accident of the previous day."

To paraphrase The Virginian's account, the balloon in which Miss Hutcheson and her pug were once again passengers darted up suddenly, struck the top of the tallest pine tree in the area and left her and her pooch dangling from a decayed limb at least 100 feet from the ground. Miss Hutcheson remained motionless, fearing that the limb might break, while her dog's yelps added to the excitement.

Finally, according to the same story, "Mr. McCartney, who had come from New York to construct the electric railroad, sent his wife to the hotel and said he would try to save the girl." As an indication of the difficulties he faced, The Virginian described the tree as being "eight feet in diameter and the lowest limb 90 feet from the ground."

Finally, after more than an hour, McCartney reached a point from which he could throw a rope to Miss Hutcheson, who was still clutching her dog. Fastening the rope around her body, Miss Hutcheson started to crawl along the limb toward the trunk of the tree, but her first move caused the limb to break and she was suspended in air.

Fortunately, the rope kept her from falling and she finally reached the ground in an unconscious state.

Despite these near tragedies, "Professor" Hutcheson, who was presumably the father of 19-year-old Ruth, persisted in making two further attempts. During the first, at which time he and Miss Hutcheson's pug were the passengers, the balloon caught fire and although Hutcheson escaped without injury the dog suffered a broken leg. This accident to the long-suffering pug finally aroused public sentiment and Hutcheson was forced to turn the dog over to the Norfolk Humane Society.

Undaunted, Hutcheson sent up a final balloon manned by another "professor" named L.N. O'Dell. This ascension turned out to be successful, for after reaching a height of about 2,000 feet, O'Dell brought his balloon down in Elmwood Cemetery.

His landing place was prophetic, however, for he was killed in 1894 in Washington, N.C., when the balloon in which he was a passenger burst and fell to the ground from 300 feet.

What happened to "Professor" Hutcheson and 19-year-old Ruth is unknown, but after their ill-fated attempts to soar into the empyrean at Ocean View in 1893, the Norfolk papers were short on balloon stories for some time thereafter.

A Rose Plucked From Peril

A flagpole sitter named Rosa Le Dareieux — yes, that was her real name and not a feeble attempt at a pun — was the unintentional heroine of the memorable tropical storm of August 22-23, 1933, that roared through the Norfolk area, leaving heavy property damage in its wake.

What is more, Rosa kept a diary while she was perched on an enclosed platform, measuring 30 inches on each side, atop a 55-foot pole overlooking Ocean View Amusement Park and a good deal of the surrounding territory.

These daily jottings were published in their entirety in The Ledger-Dispatch for August 25, 1933, and provide a good deal of fascinating information concerning the almost two months that the plucky, petite brunette had a bird's-eye view of the bright lights and vacationing crowds below.

Le Dareieux, of whom nothing further is known either before her mounting the flagpole on July 1, 1933, or her subsequent career after she was forced down by the storm, was provided by the park management with a protective cage on the pinnacle of the flagpole during the time she remained on high.

Even so, there was "hardly enough room to swing a cat," to use a time-honored saying. But Rosa's diary reveals that she made herself as comfortable as possible considering the cramped conditions.

Eventually she became so accustomed to her close quarters that she passed her time reading popular magazines hauled up by a pulley, or did a good deal of napping. She was also pleased when she learned that a waltz song, "Up in the Air With Rosa," had been composed in her honor.

Meanwhile, curious Norfolk area crowds flocked to Ocean View to gaze up in her direction, or to hear her nightly broadcasts or renditions of popular songs — one of them ironically being "Stormy Weather" — from her perch in the sky.

Rosa's diary also shows that after the first confining days she had gotten into the swing of things so well that she saw no reason not to remain in her aerie until Labor Day, the termination date for her stunt.

Her diary also includes details concerning her daily bath, "sent up in a bucket"; that she ate three hearty meals a day including all of the delicacies of the season from canteloupe to fried chicken, which she ate "exactly the way I wanted to — with my fingers"; and that her bedding was sent up to her every evening as soon as the park concessions closed and the last rubberneckers departed on the "Cinderella Express" trolley for Norfolk, Portsmouth and elsewhere.

Rosa also eventually enjoyed the fireworks that were then a nightly feature at Ocean View during the season. At first, however, she became so frightened by the rockets' red glare and bombs bursting in air that she confided to her diary, "Such banging I've never heard — each time an aerial bomb would explode my cage would quiver — and so would I."

Occasional bad weather also made Rosa uncomfortable, but as her cage was provided with a tarpaulin and side curtains, she made the best of a bad situation. On July 25, she recorded, "Raining again. Had a card from Billy West, who is buried alive on the Shore Drive, wishing me luck. He's the one who needs the luck!"

In the meantime, the granddaddy of all tropical storms in the memory of most Tidewater residents had originated some distance from the Windward Islands and traveled northwestward toward the south Atlantic coast, reaching Cape Hatteras the night of August 22-23.

According to newspaper accounts and old Norfolk Weather Bureau records, the first indication of trouble came Sunday, August 20. At 8 p.m, a torrential rain hit the area and continued all night, resulting in 6.5 inches of rainfall by 8 the next morning.

Then, after a lull, things took an ominous turn. High tides coincided with the fury of the storm, and waves along Tidewater beaches were 8 to 10 feet above normal by the following evening. What is more, for one wild moment during the blow, the Weather Bureau wind gauge in Norfolk registered 70 miles an hour.

Nevertheless, intrepid Rosa hung on for dear life atop her

55-foot flagpole. In the meantime, she saw the roof of the merry-go-round lifted, flung aloft, and hurled against the Skyrocket, one of the amusement concessions. This was followed by the unroofing of the novelty shops, the demolition of the Canals of Venice, the wrecking of the boat houses and the complete submerging of the photograph gallery.

Then, as dawn brightened and visibility became better, she was appalled to observe that the wind-driven waves were up to the boardwalk, while a few minutes later she saw the long promenade and its bulkheads smashed into splinters.

By then Rosa's flagpole perch was swaying so dangerously that Norfolk firemen stationed below feared that if it snapped it would catapult her into the rampaging waters of the Chesapeake Bay.

At that point, even though she protested vigorously, Rosa's attendant, Bill Bailey, climbed up to her perch, ordered her to catch hold of him around his neck and lock her feet around his body, and brought her down to terra firma.

But Rosa's big show wasn't over yet, for her daring rescue was such a sensational success that she and Bill Bailey repeated it every night thereafter until the park closed for the 1933 season.

Virginia First Ladies

The first ladies of the eight Virginia-born presidents were a varied lot, but only two of them were ever referred to officially by that title, which did not come into use until the second half of the 19th century. The two so designated were Ellen Louise Axson Wilson and Edith Bolling Galt Wilson, the first and second wives of Woodrow Wilson, the last native of the Old Dominion to occupy the White House.

The term "first lady" was initially applied to Lucy Ware Webb Hayes, the wife of Republican President Rutherford B. Hayes, whose term extended from 1877 to 1881. Mrs. Hayes, it will be remembered, was satirically referred to as "Lemonade Lucy" because she and her holier-than-thou husband refused to permit strong drink to be served in the White House during the four years they temporarily transformed an abode famous for its good living into a temple of piety. Their strictures, which were rigidly enforced, caused one wag to remark that water flowed like wine at the White House during the time the Hayeses presided over America's most celebrated residence.

Martha Dandridge Washington, as a faithful Anglican who believed in enjoying the good things of this world while preparing for the dubious ones of the next, would have scorned the type of religiosity later espoused by Lucy Hayes. Although Martha never lived in the White House, the executive mansions in New York and Philadelphia over which she presided for eight years as our first president's wife were well provided with rare potables and good Virginia cooking. Even so, Martha, who was formally referred to as "Lady Washington" while her husband was in office, hated being away from Mount Vernon, and went on record as saying that she felt "more like a state prisoner than anything else; there are certain bounds set for me which I must not depart from — and as I cannot do as I like, I am obstinate and stay at home a great deal."

By contrast, gregarious and social-minded Dolley Payne Todd Madison, the greatest first lady of them all, relished the political limelight. Since Thomas Jefferson was already a widower when he became president in 1801 and his two daughters regarded Washington as unhealthy, Dolley, as his intimate friend and wife of his Secretary of State, was only too happy to preside as Jefferson's hostess at the White House. Then, when her husband succeeded the Sage of Monticello, Dolley launched her own eight-year reign by opening the first inaugural ball ever held in Washington in grand style.

According to a contemporary account, Dolley, who was also known as the "Lady Presidentess," wowed the assembled company in "a pale buff-colored velvet, made plain, with a very long train, but not the least trimming, and beautiful pearl necklace, earrings and bracelets. Her headdress was a turban of the same coloured velvet and white satin (from Paris) with two superb plumes, the bird of paradise feathers."

Dolley, whom her contemporary Washington Irving described as a "fine, portly, buxom dame who has a smile and a pleasant word for everybody," was succeeded by Elizabeth Kortright Monroe, the wife of James Monroe, whose terms lasted from 1817 to 1825. Unfortunately, it was Elizabeth Monroe's lot to follow the sprightly Dolley, and her performance as first lady fell far short of the social *eclat* the White House had known during the Jefferson and Madison administrations.

Having seen a good deal of the courts of Europe while her husband filled earlier diplomatic posts for the United States abroad, Elizabeth Monroe felt Washington was provincial by comparison with the glitter she had enjoyed in Paris, London and elsewhere on the other side of the Atlantic. As a result, she was an unfortunate successor to "Queen Dolley," whose performance would have been hard to beat anyway.

Anna Symmes Harrison, the wife of William Henry Harrison, the next Virginian to be president, never made it to Washington, for her husband died one month after his inauguration. His successor, John Tyler, however, made presidential history by losing one wife and marrying another during his short term of office. Letitia Christian Tyler, his first wife, was already "in her declining years in wretched health" when she joined her husband in the White House. Then, shortly after her death, Tyler caused a good deal of chit-chat among the grande dames of the capital when he married Julia Gardiner, the "Rose of Long Island," a belle young enough to be his daughter.

Julia introduced the polka to Washington society and insisted that the Marine Band play "Hail to the Chief" whenever her doting husband entered the room on official business. She also refused to stand in her reception lines, and when guests arrived they found her regally enthroned on a carpeted dais, surrounded by maids of honor, with enough diamonds in her coiffure to create a crownlike effect.

By comparison, Margaret Smith Taylor, the wife of Virginia-born Zachary Taylor, was dowdy, but the old canard concerning her smoking a corncob pipe in the privacy of her room is untrue, as recent research shows that tobacco smoke made her "actively ill." Nevertheless, Margaret Taylor, who is said to have prayed harder for her husband's defeat than his opponents did, detested Washington and was glad to leave when Taylor died after serving only one year of his term. But that didn't stop the scandalmongers, who continued to brand her as a "poor white of the wilds" — a gross slander, as she was a daughter of a well-born Maryland planter when she married Old Rough and Ready in 1810.

Ellen Louise Axson Wilson, Woodrow Wilson's first wife, who was known as the "Angel in the White House," did not live long after her husband became president in 1913. Still, during her one year in the Executive Mansion she did what she could to alleviate the wretched lot of the poor whites and blacks who lived in the alleys within blocks of the White House. Edith Bolling Galt Wilson, the president's second wife, was a different type. A proud and beautiful ninth-generation descendant of Pocahontas and John Rolfe, the second Mrs. Wilson, though being accused of petticoat government by her enemies, had a delightful sense of humor.

Although Pocahontas, as the "darling daughter" of the "Emperor Powhatan," had been received with open arms at the English court in 1617, Mrs. Wilson had a harder time being recognized by at least one guardian of French upper-class snobbery when she was in Paris in 1919 with her husband for the Versailles Conference.

During the Wilsons' stay a duchess complained to a diplomat that the president and his wife were really very common. Coming to Mrs. Wilson's defense, the diplomat pulled a newspaper clipping from his pocket which noted that America's first lady was a descendant of Princess Pocahontas. Confronted by the evidence, the duchess then conceded that Mrs. Wilson, at least, was royalty and promptly invited her to have tea at her townhouse.

Later, Mrs. Wilson received a postcard from her mother, who was then living in Washington at the Powhatan Hotel, named for Pocahontas' father. Mrs. Wilson wanted to send the card to the duchess and tell her it was a picture of her family palace. But the president, who took his diplomatic mission to Paris seriously, called a halt to the fun and told Mrs. Wilson to hold off.

'Box' Brown's Ride to Liberty

A shining tale from a dark era is the story of how Henry Brown, a Virginia slave, escaped from bondage in 1848 in a wooden box measuring only 3 feet 1 inch long, 2 feet wide, and 2 feet 6 inches high. Brown, who was called "Box Brown" from the time of his daring exploit, dictated an account of his life — including his successful bid for freedom — a short time after his escape. Written by Charles Stearns, an abolitionist, it was published in Boston in 1849 with the title *Narrative of Henry Box Brown* and reprinted in Manchester, England, in 1861. Briefly, this was Brown's story.

Brown was born in Louisa County in 1816. He and his family were owned by a kind master who took a liking to the intelligent lad and intended to have him trained as a ploughboy or a gardener. Although Brown received decent treatment from his owner, he soon perceived the contrast between the relatively contented blacks on his master's plantation and the miserable state of many of the slaves on adjoining estates.

Brown's association with Louisa County ended when his master died in 1829. His family life was disrupted for the first time when the slaves on the plantation were divided among younger members of his former owner's family. Brown, then 13, was inherited by one of his master's sons who owned a tobacco factory in Richmond, where Brown worked for the next 19 years.

His troubles began when, instead of operating the factory himself, Brown's indolent new master employed a cruel overseer who drove his workers unmercifully in order to line his own pockets at the expense of the unsuspecting owner. Even though he was well aware of these irregularities, Brown was afraid to report them for fear of severe retribution from the overseer.

The earlier part of Brown's *Narrative* is particularly interesting for his reminiscences concerning the unmerited treatment to which Richmond's black population was subjected after the suppression of Nat Turner's Rebellion in 1831. Even so, by that time Brown had learned to keep a low profile and managed to escape being a victim of the anti-black hysteria that gripped Virginia at that time.

Troubled because of the uncertain times, Brown turned to religion for comfort. With the permission of his master he joined the Baptist Church which, unlike other Southern denominations of that time, was against slavery. Meanwhile, in some unspecified way Brown had learned to read and write, and his constant poring over the Bible, particularly the Old Testament accounts of the sufferings of the Chosen People, later lent an apocalyptic tone to the narrative he dictated as well as the anti-slavery lectures he gave both in this country and in England after his escape.

About the same time, Brown formed an acquaintance with a young black woman named Nancy who was owned by a member of the Lee family. Again, with the permission of his master, Brown married her, but his domestic life ended a few years later in tragedy. Brown and his wife were the parents of three children and as his owner let him keep part of his earnings, the couple moved into a small house of their own. But this was not for long, for one evening in August 1848 when Brown returned from work he discovered that his wife and children had been sold to a Carolina planter. When he appealed to his master for help, the latter showed his true colors by remarking cynically, "You can get another wife."

Frustrated in his efforts to regain his wife and children, Brown vowed to make a dash for freedom, trusting that his prayers would provide a solution for his problem as well as a suggestion of how his escape might be accomplished.

To quote his own words: "Suddenly, as if from above, there darted into my mind these words, 'Go and get a box, and put yourself in it.'" Luckily, Brown had a sympathetic white friend named Samuel A. Smith. When Brown appealed to him and told him of the revelation, he was instructed to obtain a small wooden packing case with the words "Right Side Up With Care" painted on it.

Smith then wrote an abolitionist friend in Philadelphia telling him to expect such a box in the near future. Once the box was obtained, Brown bored three small holes in it to prevent being suffocated. Then, after he had squeezed himself into the

cramped container, Smith nailed down the cover, addressed the
box to his Philadelphia friend and sent it to the Richmond office of
the Adams Express Company. As a precaution, Brown had taken
along only "a bladder filled with water to bathe my neck with, in
case of too great heat."

Brown's almost week-long odyssey in the wooden box
was a living nightmare.

"I was put aboard a steamboat, *and placed on my head.* In
this dreadful position, I remained the space of an hour and a half,
it seem to me, when I began to feel my eyes and head, and found
to my dismay, that my eyes were almost swollen out of their
sockets, and the veins of my temple seem ready to burst. I made
no noise however, determining to obtain '*victory or death,*' but
endured the terrible pain, as well as I could, sustained under the
whole by the thought of sweet liberty."

Fortunately, someone discovered the box was wrong side
up and righted it, after which Brown heard one of the passengers
speculate that his wooden coffin might contain a shipment of mail.
This provided Brown with the only humorous touch in his
Narrative: "Yes," thought I, "it is a *male,* indeed, although not
the *mail* of the United States."

When the steamboat reached Washington, the box was
loaded on a Philadelphia-bound freight car, at which time Brown's
temporary prison wound up again upside down. This was soon
rectified by one of the loaders, however, and Brown was finally on
the last lap of his journey to the City of Brotherly Love.

Describing his arrival, Brown recalled: "I reached the
place at three o'clock in the morning, and remained in the depot
until six o'clock, A.M., at which time a waggon drove up, and a
person inquired for a box directed to such a place, 'right side up.'
I was soon placed on this wagon, and carried to the house of my
friend's correspondent, where quite a number of persons were
waiting to receive me. There appeared to be some afraid to open
the box at first, but at length one of them rapped upon it, and with
a trembling voice, asked 'Is all right within?' to which I replied,
'All right.' The joy of these friends was excessive, and like the
ancient Jews, who repaired to the rebuilding of Jerusalem, each
one seized hold of some tool, and commenced opening my grave."

When the cover was finally off and Brown emerged, he
promptly fainted, but not for long. In concluding his memoir,

Brown expressed his incredulity at his survival like an Old Testament prophet. "Great God, was I a freeman?" he asked. "Had I indeed succeeded in effecting my escape from the human Wolves of Slavery? Long had seemed my journey, and terribly hazardous had been my attempt to gain my birth-right; but it all seemed a comparatively light price to pay for the precious boon of *Liberty.*"

Part 4: Fun and Frolic

Wit From the Pulpit

The term ecclesiastical wit is paradoxical at best, for those who are professionally qualified to battle evil are usually too preoccupied to embellish their labors with *bon mots.*

Even so, there have been a few notable exceptions among the region's clergy of the not too distant past who managed to enliven their serious duties with occasional flashes of humor. And as yarns of that sort have a way of being overlooked by more serious historians, I'd like to relate a few of the choicer ones.

For instance, take this anecdote concerning the Rev. Matthew O'Keefe, pastor of Norfolk's St. Mary's Catholic Church from 1852 to 1887.

On one occasion when Michael Glennan (1844-99) was editor of The Norfolk Virginian, he sent a young Protestant reporter to call on Father O'Keefe to see if he had any news worth printing. After knocking on O'Keefe's door, the reporter was told the reverend gentleman was in the church hearing confessions.

Being unacquainted with Catholic practice, the reporter went into the church. Figuring that Father O'Keefe was engaged in some sort of office routine, he sat in a pew and waited his turn. Finally, when he got up courage enough to enter the mysteriously dark confessional, he blurted out, "Father, I'm a reporter on The Virginian."

"That's very easily forgiven, my son," O'Keefe replied with a chuckle. "What other heinous crimes do you have to confess?"

Then there is this story, in which the Reverend Scervant Jones (1785-1854), Williamsburg's first Baptist preacher, came off with flying colors. Elder Jones, as he was known by his flock, was noted for timing his pastoral calls to coincide with the dinnertime of the members of his congregation. One day he was tardy, and when he arrived at the home of a man named Howell, he discovered that the turkey on which the family had been dining had been reduced to a meatless carcass. When asked to say a somewhat belated grace, however, Jones rose to the occasion and improvised the following:

Good Lord of Love, look from above
And bless the Howell who ate the fowl
And left the bones for Scervant Jones.

There is also this story, concerning the Right Reverend Alfred M. Randolph, the first bishop of the Episcopal Diocese of Southern Virginia, an ecclesiastical adventure that caused a good deal of merriment in Old Dominion Episcopal circles in its day.

Once when Bishop Randolph was visiting a country parish in order to administer the rite of confirmation, he was asked by his host if he would like to attend a revival meeting being held in the same community. The bishop agreed to go, and he and his host set out in a buggy.

Arriving at the tent where the service was being conducted, the bishop and his friend found the place was so crowded that they had to sit on the back row. Meanwhile, the evangelist, who was speaking on the glories of salvation, had reached that point in his sermon where he shouted, "All who want to be saved stand up!"

This brought most of his auditors to their feet, but when one of the ushers spied Bishop Randolph among the very few who still remained seated, he called out, "Stand up brother! Don't you want to go to heaven?"

"Indeed I do, my friend," the bishop replied with a twinkle in his eye, "but not tonight, thank you!"

There is also this story concerning the Right Reverend

Beverley D. Tucker, who succeeded Randolph as bishop of the Episcopal Diocese of Southern Virginia in 1918.

On one occasion when Bishop Tucker was attending a worldwide church conference in London, he and the Bishop of Michigan, a man named McCormick, arrived simultaneously at a reception that the king was giving the visiting clergy.

Taking Bishop McCormick's card first, the chamberlain squinted at the unfamiliar place name printed on it and mumbled something that sounded like "The Bishop of Mich-I-gin." Then, taking Bishop Tucker's card and recognizing the name of the first permanent British settlement in the New World printed thereon, he sang out, "The Lord Bishop of Virginia!"

At that point, Bishop Tucker tipped his fellow prelate a wink and quipped, "Ah, McCormick, why don't you come from somewhere someone has ever heard of?"

But it remained for the Right Reverend William Ambrose Brown, a former rector of St. John's Episcopal Church in Portsmouth and later bishop of the Episcopal Diocese of Southern Virginia, to drop a memorably witty blockbuster on an aloof member of the British clergy.

When Bishop Brown was in London in 1948 for a global ecclesiastical conference, he encountered a toplofty Anglican prelate at a party.

"Where are you from?" the English bishop asked condescendingly.

"From the United States," Brown replied.

"And from what diocese?" the Britisher continued.

"Southern Virginia," Brown answered obligingly.

"And where is Southern Virginia?" the British bishop inquired wearily.

"I'll tell you," Brown shot back with a mischievous smile. "Have you heard of Yorktown? Well, it's in Southern Virginia."

Ocean View of Old

Long shorn of its amusement park and eclipsed by grander waterfront tourist spots, the Ocean View of my childhood is no longer a reality. It has been obliterated by time, any number of disastrous hurricanes, and the "the tear it all down and build it bigger" syndrome.

The Ocean View I like to recall was a bayside, family-oriented resort that Norfolk boosters sixty or more years ago referred to as the "Coney Island of the South." Although by then there was a sprinkling of cottages perched on nearby dunes graced with sea oats and scrubby live oaks, Ocean View Amusement Park, the main attraction of the area, was a pleasure-oriented place dominated by an old-fashioned hotel with wide verandas punctuated with comfortable rocking chairs, a sheltered place for picnics, and an amusement casino concentrated at the north end of Granby Street that was easily accessible by trolleys (open ones in summer!) from downtown Norfolk.

Unlike Virginia Beach, which was more remote and expensive to reach, Ocean View was readily accessible to people with lighter pocketbooks. For the price of a nickel or two or a token, costing three for a quarter, it was possible for a child to exchange the heat and humidity of Norfolk, Portsmouth or Berkley for an oasis of comfort tempered by offshore breezes that made Ocean View an enchanted place even in the daytime.

If you could afford to continue your visit into the evening, the multicolored lights of the casino, the band concerts played in a Chinese pagoda-shaped stand in the midst of a lawn edged with flaming geraniums, and the almost nightly fireworks combined to transform the place into something out of the Arabian Nights.

And what fireworks they were! — not the spectacular but dull cascades of aerial pyrotechnics that are now featured throughout the Norfolk area. No, the Ocean View fireworks were truly exceptional: blazing American flags, the stars of which temporarily outshone their rivals in the heavens; gigantic portraits of George Washington as a special feature for the Fourth of July; sky-soaring replicas of the Statue of Liberty, as well as many-hued waterfalls, all bursting in air to the accompaniment of Sousa marches tooted vehemently by uniformed musicians in the bandstand.

As for the concessions along the boardwalk, what a variety they offered! There was the Old Mill Stream, later known as the Tunnel of Love, a stellar attraction for smooching couples. Then there were the games of chance where it was possible to walk away carrying a gigantic Kewpie Doll for playing a lucky number. There was also Doumar's refreshment concession where you could get a delicious baked cornucopia overflowing with the ice cream of your choice for a nickel.

And who could ever forget the gaudy, mirror-decorated merry-go-round, also known as the Flying Horses, where the lucky snagging of a brass ring could gain you a free ride on a carved and painted nag to the tune of "Dardanella" or "Over the Waves" from the concession's reedy mechanical organ, equipped with drums and cymbals for special effects?

For the venturesome there was the towering Leap-the-Dip where a super thrill as well as a fleeting bird's-eye view of the Chesapeake Bay could be had for small change. As for the beach itself, what fun it was to look for shells there or to use it as the base to erect sand castles with the aid of a tin bucket and a miniature shovel.

I'd like to end on an upbeat note by including a jingle based on an incident that reputedly began on an Ocean View trolley of my youth. It's probably apocryphal, but who cares, for it's the fun that counts. Read it, laugh and remember!

Two pickpockets met on an Ocean View car, each picking the other's pocket.

The woman crook got his pocketbook, the man got her diamond locket.

Admiring each other, they fell in love, they married, but what was worse,

They wished for a child who could snag a bag, or pilfer a Scotsman's purse.

Their wish came true, and a boy was born, a slick-looking,

sly-faced mite,
     But alas, alack, with a crippled hand — the fingers were closed up tight.
     The heartbroken parents hurried the child to a famous specialist,
     And offered him watches and precious gems, if he could unclench the fist.
     First thing he did was to tie a string to a wristwatch with jeweled band,
     And wave it steadily, back and forth, just over the crippled hand.
     As the fingers opened, the mother and dad began to dance and sing,
     For there in the palm of the baby's hand was the midwife's diamond ring!

Gems From Old Virginia

For years, I have been toying with the pleasurable idea of compiling an anthology of Virginia humor from the founding of Jamestown in 1607 until the present.

Having let the years slip by without doing anything constructive about it, however, I am beginning to believe it might be a good idea to use an occasional column as a showcase for some of the choicer gems of Old Dominion wit that I have collected.

In that way I should at least be able to share some of the more outstanding examples before my time comes to take "a great leap in the dark," to use an old Thomas Hobbes speculative expression.

To get down to business, I thought I had heard and laughed at, all of the smug old FFV bromides until I recently encountered the following top-drawer example.

During a conversation between two grande dames, one from the Old Dominion, the other from the Tar Heel State, the subject of the First Families of Virginia came up.

At that point, the matron from south of what Colonel William Byrd II somewhat condescendingly referred to as the "Dividing Line" enquired, "What became of the Second Families of Virginia?"

"Why, I'm surprised that you ask," the lady from the commonwealth replied airily. "Who do you suppose populated North Carolina?"

To give the other side a fair chance at a rebuttal, it took a citizen of North Carolina to puncture Virginia's much vaunted superiority.

Once when reflecting on the adamant attitude of latter-day Virginia Tories against any change from tradition, Josephus Daniels, the celebrated North Carolina journalist and statesman, hit the nail squarely on the head when he declared, "Virginia was the cradle and the graveyard of democracy."

Still another delightfully accurate potshot at Virginia toploftiness was scored in the following anecdote.

A Virginian, who had gone to North Carolina on some sort of business, fell gravely ill. Several doctors were called in for a consultation, but none of them was able to diagnose the case.

Then one of them arrived at a conclusion, but was afraid to voice his speculation as the ailment, as he regarded it, was of the utmost rarity.

Finally, when he was pressed by his colleagues to put his diagnosis into to words, he stroked his chin gravely and replied, "Gentlemen, this man is suffering from something that has never been encountered before in the annals of medicine." Then, after a dramatic pause, he declared, "He is a Virginian with an inferiority complex!"

Then there is this observation by the late Colgate W. Darden concerning the alcohol problem from which many members of the Virginia bar have blissfully suffered since time immemorial.

When Darden, whose wit was like a rapier in a silken sheath, was governor of Virginia, he quipped on one occasion, "They come out of law school at the university with a good education, and they go back to the county and sit around waiting for cases with nothing to do but search a title now and then. No wonder many of them wind up wedded to the bottle."

While we are in the groves of academe, here is another gem that deserves to be passed down to posterity. When Dr. Francis Pendleton Gaines, the president of Washington and Lee University, was about to speak at an important function, he was introduced by an old college chum.

"My friends, I know a lot about Dr. Gaines," he began, "but I will not waste the time by telling you anything except that he is the seventh son and eleventh child of his parents."

At that point, someone in the audience commented loudly, "My God! I'd hate to take that guy on in a crap game!"

Finally, there is this crown jewel of Virginia chauvinistic oratory that has become one of the legends at Mr. Jefferson's university.

On the occasion of a visit by President Grover Cleveland to the University of Virginia, he was introduced by General

Fitzhugh Lee, who later served as governor of Virginia. Lee, a loyal son of the Old Dominion, had no intention of seeing the prolific Mother of Presidents deposed by anyone.

"Mr. President," he began graciously, "we are indeed honored in welcoming you to Virginia today, both as a loyal Democrat and the president of the United States. In fact, it has been a long time since we have had a president with us."

Then, fearing that such praise might turn Cleveland's head, Lee added the following, much to the delight of his audience:

"But the time has been, suh," he declared with a histrionic gesture, "when we could go out on this very old rotunda porch and holler, 'Mr. President!' — and the woods would be full of 'em!"

Tart Tongues and Tourists

During the past 50 years, tourism has poured millions of dollars into the coffers of a commonwealth that proudly endorses the slogan that "Virginia Is for Lovers." In the wake of this golden Niagara, however, the influx of out-of-state visitors also has attracted countless gadders who gad for the sake of gadding, most of whom have left the Old Dominion as ignorant of its people and customs as they were before they dropped by for a visit.

Fortunately, most of those who act as guides to the historic homes and other storied places throughout the commonwealth are endowed with keen senses of humor, and the gaffes they overhear from tourists, or even commit themselves while carrying out their duties, are rapidly becoming a specialized field of Virginia folklore.

Colonial Williamsburg, as the state's stellar tourist attraction, is high on the list of backdrops for such anecdotes. So to start the ball rolling, it might be a good idea to begin with a few yarns from that area.

Not long ago, two ladies from England were standing with a group of visiting dignitaries on the front steps of the Governor's Palace when an oxcart, one of the picturesque stage props of the restored colonial capital, was driven down Palace Green by a man in 18th century costume.

"What on earth are those strange creatures?" one of the women exclaimed, pointing to the lumbering team of oxen that drew the cart.

"Oh, don't be silly, dear," her companion trumpeted, "those are American buffalos, two of the few remaining survivors of an almost extinct breed."

On another occasion, after a hostess had pointed out a prized antique Chinese cricket cage on a mantel in the Palace, she was taken aback when an irate matron in the party she had been conducting exploded, "Well, if those royal governors didn't have anything better to do than to listen to crickets chirp, no wonder George Washington fought the Revolution!"

Most colonial dwellings have a problem accommodating tourists with bathroom facilities, and there was one occasion when the suggestion by one of the Palace hostesses — a dignified lady of British origin — backfired. When a woman sightseer asked to be directed to a restroom, the hostess suggested the questioner use the facilities of the nearby restored Brush-Everard House. In making her suggestion, however, the hostess remarked somewhat ambiguously, "The Palace restrooms are so inconveniently located in the garden that I feel it would be easier for you to go to the Brush."

At that point the horrified tourist shot back, "Listen here, madam, I'm a lady, and no matter how badly I have to go, I'll never do that!"

Still another Palace guide reported overhearing the following remark made by a dowager after she had been escorted through the sumptuous ballroom: "Girls," the somewhat musically mixed-up woman exclaimed, "can't you just imagine all of those lovely colonial beaux and belles dancing the minuet here to the strains of 'The Blue Danube Waltz'!"

There is also the tale about another Williamsburg hostess who paused at the door of the House of Burgesses after showing a large party around only to be tapped on the shoulder by a bosomy matron in a large, flowered hat. "Thank you, my dear, for showing me my ancestral home," the posy-crowned woman cooed. "You know, my mother was a Burgess!"

Switching the scene to Yorktown, there was the occasion when one of the guides there momentarily forgot the name of the tune ("The World Turned Upside Down") that the regimental bands played during the British surrender in 1781.

While he was trying to recall it, a little old lady in the crowd came up with this bit of musical misinformation. "It was 'The Star Spangled Banner,' she chirped brightly. "That was the first time it was ever played in public, you know."

As for the Richmond scene, there was the time a guide was escorting a party of first-graders through St. Paul's Episcopal Church on Capitol Square. After giving the building's history, she ended her spiel by pointing out the pew in which Jefferson Davis, the president of the Confederacy, was seated when General Lee's courier arrived with the news that the city had to be evacuated. When she thought that had sunk in sufficiently, the guide asked if there were any questions.

"Yes, ma'am," a pert little girl in the party piped up. "Did he have to go to the john?"

To wind things up, there was the memorable occasion when a young female descendant of one of Virginia's most distinguished families was showing a party of sightseers, from north of the Mason and Dixon Line, through her ancestral home during Historic Garden Week.

When she paused in her narration, a belligerent male tourist in the group asked in a twangy Down East accent to see the bullwhip that, he said, he had heard the young lady's ancestors used to cow their servants before the Emancipation Proclamation.

"Oh, that one was stolen by a no 'count Yankee scoundrel during the War Between the States," the quick-thinking young lady flashed back. "But I've got a replacement on order right now to use on mouthy contemporary carpetbaggers like yourself when they get out of line!"

Through a Glass Wetly

Maybe I am guilty of provincial snobbery, but it seems to me that Virginia humor of an alcoholic variety has a headier bouquet than competitive vintages distilled by the other 49 states. Perhaps this is because the social life of the Old Dominion was nurtured over a long period by an Anglican tolerance that recommended the advisability of wetting one's whistle on any occasion, a deeply rooted tradition that still maintains that when four Episcopalians are gathered together, there will always be a fifth.

Even so, after having devoted almost a lifetime to collecting and evaluating Virginia tippling yarns, I am convinced there is a refreshing irreverence about the commonwealth's bacchanalian wit that is uniquely urbane as well as down to earth.

For instance, take the following exchange between Ellen Glasgow, the author of some of Virginia's most delightful social satires, and a waggish Richmond policeman that took place during that regrettable period of American history known as Prohibition.

Miss Glasgow's handsome Greek Revival house, in which she lived most of her life, was in a once-fashionable neighborhood of the Holy City that had gradually deteriorated into a slum. When, on the occasion of the anecdote, the policeman twitted Miss Glasgow for continuing to reside in an area that had become the heart of Richmond's bootleg district, she airily reminded him that it was rather strange for a conscientious officer of the law to even admit that there was such a thing as an alcoholic oasis in Virginia's technically bone-dry capital.

When that had sunk in, she laughingly added that she was considerably consoled, however, to know that anything as low-life as a bootlegging district actually had a heart.

There is also the story concerning a witty rejoinder of Chief Justice John Marshall, whose cellar was one of the best-stocked spirituous depositories in the Old Dominion of his time.

Upon learning on one occasion that it was being whispered that the justices of the Supreme Court were imbibing too freely, the members of that august body decided they would henceforth drink nothing on their weekly consultation days unless it was raining.

When the next consultation rolled around, Marshall asked Joseph Story, an associate justice, to go to the window and see if there was any sign of a shower.

Story reported, "Mr. Chief Justice, I have carefully examined the case and I have to give it as my opinion that there is not the slightest sign of rain."

At that point, the thirsty Marshall replied sternly, "Justice Story, I think that is the shallowest and most illogical opinion I have ever heard you deliver," adding: "You forget that our jurisdiction is as broad as the Republic. Therefore, by the laws of nature it must be raining some place in our bailiwick."

Then, with a wink and a broad smile, Marshall called out, "Waiter, bring on the rum!"

There is also the tale of an alcoholic Tidewater lawyer who habitually deposited his cast-off bottles in the basement of his house.

Some time after the death of his wife, he requested a plumber to fix his furnace, but before that could be accomplished the cellar had to be cleared of two truckloads of "dead soldiers," to use a time-honored Tidewater euphemism for empty liquor receptacles.

This situation was reported by the plumber to his wife, who collared the lawyer the next Sunday as he was leaving church.

"You should be ashamed of yourself," she trumpeted. "Your constant boozing is certainly not setting a good example for your motherless children."

Then coming to the point, she reported what her husband had told her, ending with the rhetorical question, "Where on earth did all of those empty bottles come from?"

"Damned if I know," the lawyer shot back. "I never bought an empty liquor bottle in my life!"

Then there is this delightful yarn from the repetoire of Rear Admiral Cary T. Grayson, President Wilson's personal physician.

Grayson was a native of Culpeper, where many of the inhabitants formerly went in for distilling moonshine liquor in a big way.

On one occasion, according to Grayson, a leading citizen who had recently been elected county prosecutor, was taking a horseback ride through the hills. Noticing some suspicious smoke up a hillside, he also became aware of a small boy playing beside the road.

"Sonny," he asked, "is that a still up there?"

"It mought be, or it moughtn't," the boy answered.

"Are you by any chance a lookout for it?" the prosecutor inquired.

"I mought be and I moughtn't," the boy drawled.

"Well," the prosecutor remarked, "you hold my horse while I go up there and investigate."

The boy obediently took the horse's bridle, and the prosecutor climbed the fence and started across a meadow toward the smoke on the hillside.

When he had gone a little way, the boy called out, "Hey, mister!"

"What is it?" yelled the prosecutor.

"Well, eff'n you don't come back," the boy asked, "what must I do with the horse?"

The Famous First UFO

Virginia has a good many historical firsts to its credit. Our forefathers were the first Englishmen to invade these shores, although genealogical purists now say this was no distinction as the immigration restrictions were later more stringent. Be that as it may, we still had the first legislative assembly in what is now the United States at Jamestown in 1619. What is more, we gave the country its first president, etc., etc.

Now, another heretofore unsuspected first has been added. Briefly, a son of the Old Dominion not only saw, but graphically described, what appears to have been the first unidentified flying object, or UFO, in American history. The proof of this assertion turned up recently in a letter in the Jefferson Papers in the Library of Congress, claiming that a spectacular UFO was sighted over Norfolk County (now the City of Chesapeake) on the night of July 25, 1813.

UFO sightings throughout Virginia have been relatively frequent in recent times, but until this earlier report was rediscovered, Virginia historians were too busy recounting the derring-do of the state's earlier citizenry during the Revolution or The Late Unpleasantness to devote their attention to aerial phenomena.

According to a listing of UFO sightings covering the period from 1868 to 1968, printed in *Passport to Magonia: From Folklore to Flying Saucers*, by Jacques Vallee (1969), seven UFOs were observed in the commonwealth during the period embracing 1965-67. Interestingly, the first one was a Norfolk sighting. On January 14, 1965, James Myers told of seeing a bright circular silver object rise from the ground and take off at high speed.

Five days later, a workman cutting wood on the Augusta archery range saw two saucer-shaped objects hovering in the sky. The smaller one landed, a door opened and three figures emerged. These looked human, but had reddish-orange skin and staring eyes, while one of them had "a long finger on his left hand."

The workman added that their clothes were the same color as their craft, the open door of which revealed an eerie light inside. The craft was described as so highly polished it would have been visible at 5,000 feet on a clear day. Climaxing this particular sighting, the observer stated that the occupants uttered sounds which he could not understand. They also re-entered the craft by a door, the outline of which could not be seen when it was closed.

Space does not permit further descriptions of the other five Virginia sightings mentioned in Vallee's book, as well as others recorded since that time, but all of them were as spectacular as the Augusta archery range sighting. Even so, the 1813 UFO recorded by the Norfolk County man easily matched all of the recent Virginia-oriented ones described in Vallee's book and elsewhere, plus humorous touches lacking in the others. So, first a word concerning the man who saw the aerial object and reported it to Thomas Jefferson.

Edward Hansford, the man who reported the UFO in 1813 over what is now Chesapeake, was a member of an old York County family that acquired notoriety in 1676 when one of its members, Major Thomas Hansford, was hanged by Sir William Berkeley for the traitorous role he played in Bacon's Rebellion.

The later Hansford, a carpenter, was living in Norfolk County during the Revolution, working on forts erected by the Commonwealth. In 1784, he married Ann Kidd in Norfolk County. In 1802, he was appointed harbormaster for the District of Norfolk and Portsmouth.

At the time of the sighting, Hansford operated the Washington Tavern on London Street in Portsmouth, the sign of which depicted the Father of Our Country commanding his troops on one side and planting a field on the other. When Hansford died is not known, but his widow survived until 1832, running a fashionable boarding house on East Main Street in Norfolk where in 1824 she was Lafayette's hostess.

So much for prologue. The following is the significant excerpt from Hansford's letter to Jefferson, dated Portsmouth, July 31, 1813, in which he described the strange object that he and a Baltimore citizen named John L. Clark witnessed.

"We the subscribers most earnestly solicit, that your honor will give us your opinion on the following extraordinary phenomenon viz.: At (the exact time is omitted in the letter) hour on the night of the 25th instant, we saw in the South a Ball of fire as full as large as the sun at Maridian (sic) which was frequently obscured within the space of ten minutes by a smoke emitted from its own body, but ultimately retained its briliancy, and form during that period, but with apparent agitation. It then assumed the form of a turtle which also appeared to be much agitated and as frequently obscured by a similar smoke. It descended obliquely to the West, and raised again perpendicular to its original hite (sic) which was on or about 75 degrees. It then assumed the shape of a human skeleton which was frequently obscured by a like smoke and as frequently descended and ascended - It then assumed the form of a Scotch Highlander arrayed for battle and extremely agitated, and ultimately passed to the West and disappeared in its own smoke."

Whether Jefferson answered Hansford's letter is now unknown, but one thing is certain: The liquor provided by the Washington Tavern must have been pretty potent. Otherwise, how can we account for Hansford's transformation of what apparently was a legitimate UFO into a human skeleton or a Scotch Highlander?

The Mythical Pallbearer

When Dr. Edmund Helder died in Stafford County, no one suspected he would one day be accorded the unmerited distinction of having been one of Shakespeare's pallbearers. The incident, which forcefully illustrates how false rumors frequently temporarily overshadow unvarnished history, is one of Virginia's most fascinating and little-known tales.

Before I recount the zany details it might be a good idea to include a few facts concerning the historical Dr. Helder, if for no other reason than to show that it would have been impossible for him to have assisted at Shakespeare's burial in 1616.

Born in England during the early part of the 17th century, Helder was a son of Richard Helder (d. 1669) of the parish of Little Staughton in Bedfordshire. So numerous were the elder Helder's sons that he found it expedient to bind several of them out as apprentices. Thus, in 1657, young Edmund was apprenticed for an eight-year term to the London apothecary William Royston. After completing his indenture, Edmund Helder came to Virginia, where he became a "practitioner in physic and chyrurgery" (as surgeons were called then) and practiced until his death in Stafford County in 1678.

So much for solid history. Now for an excursion into the wild blue yonder of fanciful and sentimental speculation.

In 1865, Moncure D. Conway, a native of Stafford County then serving as the minister of South Place Unitarian Chapel in London, wrote an article titled "Virginia, First and Last," which was published in Fraser's Magazine. In it, he emphatically stated that the churchyard of St. George's Episcopal Church in Fredericksburg contained a tombstone bearing an inscription to the effect that it marked the grave of a man who had been a pallbearer for William Shakespeare. This assertion was immediately challenged by British Shakespeare authorities. Conway backtracked and admitted that his authority for the statement had been included in a recently received letter from a now unidentifiable fellow Virginian.

Conway promised to investigate the matter further, however, and was somewhat abashed when subsequent enquiries among Fredericksburg antiquaries resulted in the discovery that no such stone existed. Even so, Conway's mother later forwarded him a clipping from an 1870 New York newspaper that not only insisted that the stone was located in St. George's Cemetery in Fredericksburg but printed the epitaph, presumably copied a few years earlier by a correspondent who was passing through the town.

The alleged inscription, which subsequent investigation proved was romantic fiction, read: "Here lies the body of Edward (sic) Helder, practitioner in Physic Chyrurgery. Born in Bedfordshire, England, in the year of our Lord 1541 — was contemporary with, and one of the Pallbearers of William Shakespeare. After a brief illness his spirit ascended in the year of our Lord 1618, aged 76."

Armed with this information as well as numerous other notices concerning the Helder epitaph which began appearing periodically in newspapers throughout the United States, Conway attempted to track down the elusive tombstone while on periodic visits to Virginia from 1870 onward. Then, after his permanent return to the United States in 1885, he began a systematic search of the Fredericksburg area for Dr. Helder's tombstone.

By then he had convinced himself that Helder's supposed role as a Shakespeare pallbearer was dubious. Being a dedicated amateur historian and antiquary, however, he still felt that the assertion that had gotten him into hot water with British Shakespeareans had some basis in reality even if the pallbearer business was a fanciful addition to the career of a man which the records showed had lived in Stafford County during the latter part of the 17th century.

Beginning with St. George's Episcopal Cemetery and the Masonic Graveyard in Fredericksburg, Conway inspected every tombstone in those places that bore the slightest resemblance to what the national press notices had begun to describe as a "red sandstone" slab on which the epitaph was supposedly chiseled. Drawing a blank, Conway extended his search into the surrounding countryside where he eventually encountered a tradition concerning the former existence of an ancient granite tombstone that once marked the grave of someone with the surname of Helder.

Conway finally located a small fragment of the formerly massive stone that had marked Dr. Helder's grave near a place called Potomac Creek. By that time, however, age and neglect had practically obliterated what little lettering remained, but that did not discourage Conway.

Learning that a former Union soldier, C.J. Brown of Byfield, Mass., had been stationed during the Civil War near where the fragment of Dr. Helder's tombstone was discovered, Conway sent him a map of the Potomac Creek neighborhood with a request for any facts that he might be able to recall concerning the stone when it was in a better state of preservation.

Brown replied that he had indeed been stationed in the Potomac Creek area with the Sixth New Hampshire Volunteers in August 1862, at which time he had discovered the badly mutilated Helder tombstone. He also confirmed his familiarity with the area by precisely marking the spot on the map where Conway had discovered the fragment of the tombstone more than 20 years later. Brown then described the already battered stone as it had appeared in 1862, and also included a copy he had made of what remained of the Helder epitaph at the same time.

Unfortunately, Brown was unacquainted with the peculiarities of British 17th century lapidary lettering and numerals, and among other misreadings, he jotted down 1618, rather than 1678, as the year Helder died. Since Brown's copy of Helder's epitaph, imperfect and incorrect as it was, made no mention of the doctor's having been one of Shakespeare's pallbearers, Conway got around that problem somewhat lamely in a later article in Harper's New Monthly Magazine (January 1886) titled "Hunting a Mythical Pall-Bearer."

In it, he wrote: "It is possible that some correspondent (other than Brown) having copied the epitaph...added that Dr. Helder was a contemporary of Shakespeare and might have attended his funeral. A printer may have incorporated the comment in the epitaph and some contemporary evolved the simple statement into the startling one."

To sum up the matter, as Shakespeare was born in 1564 and died in 1616, Dr. Helder, who was born some time during the

early 17th century and died in 1678, could hardly have been a
pallbearer for the Bard. Even so, the overzealousness of
untrained antiquarians and Conway's uncritical reporting of their
questionable findings have combined to create a delightful off-beat
Virginia tale plus a salutary lesson for those who feel that
historical facts are improved by fanciful embroidery. As usual,
Shakespeare said it best when in *Twelfth Night* he admonished:
"Thus the whirligig of time brings in his revenges."

A Shakespeare Comedy

To brush up on our Shakespeare, let us recall an episode in Williamsburg in 1938 that attempted to denigrate his long-established reputation.

The facts are available in *Foundations Unearthed,* a pamphlet published in 1974 by Veritas Press of Los Angeles, which in turn was an updated version of an earlier booklet, *Francis Bacon's Great Virginia Vault,* first issued in 1940.

The author, Mrs. Marie Bauer Hall, who identified herself as Mrs. Marie Bauer at the time she was active in Williamsburg, was by 1948 a staff member of the First Temple and College of Astrology in Los Angeles. Before assuming the post, she had married Manly P. Hall, a mystic. Long before becoming Hall's wife, however, Mrs. Bauer had concluded that Sir Francis Bacon, the famous Elizabethan and Jacobean statesman and scholar, was not only the chief collaborator in the authorship of Shakespeare's plays, but that Shakespeare was illiterate and therefore incapable of writing the works attributed to him.

These convictions assumed greater urgency in Mrs. Bauer's imagination in 1938, when she entered upon a detailed analysis of *A Collection of Emblems Ancient and Modern,* an anthology of verses and engravings compiled by George Wither, a contemporary of Bacon and Shakespeare, published in 1635. Concentrating her cryptographic skills on presumed enigmatic allusions to Elizabethan and Jacobean worthies in Wither's book, Mrs. Bauer arrived at some startling conclusions, none of which have any basis in recorded history.

Mrs. Bauer claimed that Queen Elizabeth I and her favorite, the Earl of Leicester, were secretly married and that Elizabeth gave birth to a boy who was entrusted to Sir Nicholas Bacon, the lord keeper of the great seal, who named him Francis Bacon and reared him as his own son. This boy, according to Mrs. Bauer, grew up to be the celebrated Sir Francis Bacon.

But there were other esoteric arrows in Mrs. Bauer's quiver, for according to her reckonings Elizabeth and Leicester were later the parents of the impetuous Earl of Essex, whom Elizabeth had beheaded for treason in 1601. Earlier, according to Mrs. Bauer, Essex had become his mother's lover and helped her to murder Leicester, the man who had not only sired him, but was also the father of Sir Francis Bacon.

As if this were not complicated enough, Mrs. Bauer further asserted that when Sir Francis Bacon reached maturity and was recognized as one of the greatest intellects of his time, he headed a literary clique which not only wrote the plays credited to Shakespeare, using thinly veiled contemporary political episodes for their plots, but also bribed Shakespeare, an ignorant actor, to claim their authorship to protect the real authors from prosecution for libel.

Meanwhile, Mrs. Bauer came up with two other things concerning Sir Francis Bacon that steered her thoughts in the direction of the Old Dominion.

First, she claimed that Sir Francis had created the philosophical groundwork on which the Constitution of the United States was later based. Second, Sir Francis had sired a son whom he unaccountably named Henry Blount. This nebulous character reportedly came to Jamestown in 1635 after Sir Francis' death, bringing along his father's papers, including the proof that he had masterminded the writing of the plays attributed to Shakespeare.

These documents, according to Mrs. Bauer, were sealed in copper cylinders and buried by Blount around 1675 in three places — at Bacon's Castle in Surry County, at an unspecified spot on the James River, but principally in Williamsburg. Incredibly, Mrs. Bauer went on to assert that Blount changed his name to Nathaniel Bacon in 1676 and became the leader of what is known in Virginia history as Bacon's Rebellion.

Mrs. Bauer's conviction that Williamsburg was the main repository for Bacon's manuscripts was derived from a cryptogram in Wither's book which she deciphered thus: "Under the first brick church in Williamsburg, Va., lies Francis Bacon's vault." How Wither, who died in 1667, more than 30 years before Williamsburg was established, came up with this before-the-fact prophecy was not explained in Mrs. Bauer's treatise.

Armed with these arcane assumptions, Mrs. Bauer

arrived in Williamsburg late in May 1938, and after a good deal of preliminary poking around Bruton Parish churchyard she requested an audience with the vestry of the church. When that was granted, she informed the group that the land beneath their church (erected in 1712-15) held not only the key to the authorship of Shakespeare's plays, but also the proof that Sir Francis Bacon, as the firstborn of Queen Elizabeth I, had been the lawful heir to the crown of England.

While the befuddled vestrymen were trying to take that in, Mrs. Bauer requested their permission to dig under the tower of the church, claiming that a "Great Virginia Vault" containing the copper cylinders would be found there. Her wish was granted, but when a nine-foot shaft had been dug and nothing was found, the vestry hastily rescinded its permission before the tower collapsed into the hole. But that didn't stop Mrs. Bauer.

Until then, she had believed the foundations she was seeking were beneath the existing church, but her subsequent deciphering of supposedly cabalistic symbols carved on certain tombstones in the churchyard, as well as the consultation of an ancient plat of the town, convinced her they were adjacent to the present edifice.

A second request to dig was denied, but that didn't deter Mrs. Bauer from probing around the area with a long iron rod. Finally, she discovered what she was seeking, but it should be mentioned that the vestry as well as officials of Colonial Williamsburg were already aware that the foundations of the earlier brick Bruton Parish Church, built in 1685, were somewhere beneath the surface of the present graveyard.

From then on, the affair became unadulterated slapstick that the Bard of Avon would undoubtedly have relished.

Shortly after her divining rod had struck something solid, Mrs. Bauer visited the churchyard early one morning accompanied by a band of enthusiastic helpers and sensation seekers. By the time a vestryman sauntered by and saw dirt flying in the air, part of the foundation of the earlier Bruton Parish Church had been uncovered. A hastily convened vestry meeting put a stop to the digging, but by then the press had gotten wind of what was going on, and the story soon became national news.

The discovery of the foundation of the 1685 church more or less intimidated the vestry and the town officials into appropriating funds to uncover the entire foundation. But when this was done and no "Great Virginia Vault" turned up containing Sir Francis Bacon's papers, particularly the proof that he had masterminded the authorship of Shakespeare's plays, the vestry called an immediate halt to the digging. Then, after the measurements of the foundation had been taken and recorded, the uncovered brickwork was covered over again.

As for Mrs. Bauer, she reluctantly left Williamsburg, her mission unfulfilled. But after abandoning her divining rod she took up her pen, and her booklet, which by 1974 had gone into a fourth printing, stoutly maintained her belief that the writings of Sir Francis Bacon, and particularly the fact that Shakespeare was only a "Stratford clown," still remained stashed away in a "Great Virginia Vault" beneath the tree-shaded graveyard of Bruton Parish Church in Williamsburg.

Take My Mother-in-Law...

Although Mother-in-Law Day, which was dreamed up (or should I say was conceived during a nightmare?) in 1934 by Gene Howe, an Amarillo, Texas, newspaper editor, it has still not caught on sufficiently as an American holiday to be celebrated with fanfares. Even so, it is good to know how Howe came up with the idea which continues to pay tribute to those American mothers-in-law who have the good grace to endure the bad publicity that has been aimed at their particular sphere of womanhood from time immemorial.

Now don't get the idea that I'm going to devote the entire column to the aggressive battleaxes who have given themselves a bad name by the constant interference in the everyday doings of their married sons and daughters. No, that would be unfair to the good mothers-in-law who, through the ages, have had the sense to back off from their offspring's lives once they have left the nest.

To present both sides of the question, however, it will be necessary to toss in a little pertinent evidence concerning those who, according to no less authority than *Ann Landers' Encyclopedia,* are responsible for the "in-law problems which still figure prominently as one of the major causes of marital bust-ups."

The Roman poet Juvenal went on record around 12 A.D. as saying: "Give up all hope of peace so long as your mother-in-law is alive." The New Testament (Luke XII, 53) also avers: "The mother-in-law (shall be divided) against her daughter-in-law, and the daughter-in-law against her mother-in-law." Francois Parfaict (1698-1753), the French historian, declared: "Of all men, Adam was the happiest; he had no mother-in-law." Further, an old Japanese proverb warns: "Never rely on the glory of the morning or on the smile of your mother-in-law."

H.L. Mencken, the Sage of Baltimore, even declared that

"Conscience is a mother-in-law whose visit never ends," while Leonard Louis Levinson in his *Webster's Unafraid Dictionary* adds to the hilarity by defining a mother-in-law as "The other woman in many a domestic triangle" or "One who frequently goes too far by remaining too near." Still another modern wit, Laurence Peter, has gone on record with "Admitting a mistake to my mother-in-law is like bleeding in front of a shark." Finally, an anonymous contemporary wag maintains: "Happiness is seeing your mother-in-law's picture on the back of a milk carton."

Switching to illustrative anecdotes, I recall an old Berkley yarn concerning a heated set-to between a couple of Southside newlyweds, at the culmination of which the wife wailed, "Oh, if I had only taken Mother's advice and never married you!" At that revelation, the husband smote his forehead and exclaimed, "Did your mother really try to prevent our marriage?" "Yes!", his better half shot back after which the husband groaned, "How I have been wronging that good woman!"

Then there is the old Norfolk story of an incident at a fashionable wedding. When a formidable dowager bore down on an usher and demanded to be taken to her seat, he asked, "Are you a friend of the bridegroom?" "Certainly not," the matron replied icily, "I am the bride's mother."

Let's take a look at the favorable aspects of the mother-in-law question. Returning to the Bible for an affirmative reference, there is no more perfect example anywhere than the mother-in-law daughter-in-law relationship that existed between Naomi and Ruth. Turning to early England, one of the Paston Letters, dating from 1477, contains this tribute from a contented son-in-law: "I trow ther is not a kynder woman leveng then I shall have to my modyr in lawe."

Switching to Virginia, there are several notable examples of friendly relationships between celebrated sons and daughters of the Old Dominion and their mothers-in-law. For instance, there was the most amiable empathy between Dolley Madison, the sprightly wife of James Madison, the Father of the Constitution, and her husband's mother, Mrs. Eleanor Conway Madison. All three lived in close intimacy at Montpelier, the Madison estate in Orange County, for almost half a century after Madison and Dolley were married in 1794, and the association was notable for its longstanding, good-humored tolerance.

Matoaks als Rebecka daughter to the mighty Prince
Powhatan Emperour of Attanoughskomouck als virginia
converted and baptized in the Christian faith, and
wife to the worth Mr. Joh Rolff.

Pocahontas

The Earl of Southampton (1573-1624) and his cat.

James I

William Shakespeare

Sarah Harrison Blair
Courtesy of the Muscarelle Museum of Art,
College of William and Mary

Col. Daniel Parke
Courtesy of the Virginia Historical Society

Daniel Parke Custis

Courtesy of
Washington/Custis/Lee
Collection,
Washington and Lee
University,
Lexington, Va.

George Washington

Courtesy of
Washington/Custis/Lee
Collection
Washington and Lee
University,
Lexington, Va.

Thomas Jefferson

Dolley Madison

25   THE PRINCE OF WALES, 1859
from the painting by Winterhalter

Edward VII as Prince of Wales

William Short

Courtesy of
Muscarelle Museum
of Art,
College of
William and Mary

John Marshall

James Armistead Lafayette
Courtesy of Valentine Museum,
Richmond

Edgar Allen Poe

Gen. and Mrs. George E. Pickett

Robert E. Lee death mask
Courtesy,
Confederate Museum,
Richmond, Va.

Abraham Lincoln

3 feet 1 inch long, 2 feet wide, 2 feet 6 inches high.

Henry "Box" Brown
(1816- ?)
and his means
to freedom

The Rt. Rev.
William
Ambrose
Brown

Trinity's
controversial
window

Lord Louis
Mountbatten

Then there was the pleasantly close relationship between Robert E. Lee and his mother-in-law, Mrs. Mary Lee Randolph Fitzhugh Custis. Not only did Mrs. Custis encourage the match between her daughter and the impecunious young Lee, but after their marriage she became a valued friend and mentor to the man who was later familiarly and fondly known as Marse Robert.

Finally, there was the case of George Washington, who was so fond of his mother-in-law, Mrs. Frances Jones Dandridge, that he cordially invited her to reside with his wife and himself at Mount Vernon. It is worthy of note, however, that Mrs. Dandridge, an elegant, fun-loving 18th century dame, was in direct contrast to Mary Ball Washington, George's domineering, constantly complaining and not particularly sociable mother. In any event, the Father of His Country emphatically discouraged his mother from ever trying to take up residence in his home. The particulars, including Washington's chilly letter to his disagreeable parent suggesting that she remain under her own roof in Fredericksburg, can easily be found in Douglas Southall Freeman's monumental biography of the Squire of Mount Vernon.

Querulous old Mary Ball Washington has had her posthumous revenge, however, for not only has she been deified by sentimental biographers who have little regard for the truth, but her home is now maintained as a shrine. Meanwhile, Washington's pleasant mother-in-law is forgotten. Even so, there are those who visit Fredericksburg annually who see the irony of the situation, and two of these irreverent tourists, who merely designated themselves as V.H.A. and D.A., were so amused when they saw the sign "The Home of Mary Mother of Washington 1753-1788" affixed to Washington's mother's home that they penned this parody on the Christmas carol "Oh Little Town of Bethlehem." It goes like this:

Oh little Town of Fredericksburg,
How pilgrims to thee hie!
Past neon signs the juke box whines
As tourist cars go by.
Come see **THE HOME OF MARY**
All hallowed with fresh paint -
Plus local dames in hoop skirt frames:
Quintessence of the quaint!

Time To Chuckle

Henry Wheeler Shaw (1818-85), the 19th century American literary maverick whose witty writings under the nom de plume of Josh Billings kept our great-grandparents in stitches, once quipped: "Laughter is the sensation of feeling good all over and showing it principally in one place."

That being a truth universally acknowledged by anyone who is not a confirmed sourpuss, I'd like to present a few choice examples of Old Dominion waggery.

Let's begin with a yarn dating from the time that unreconstructed Southerners still refer to as The Late Unpleasantness. When General John Bankhead Magruder (1810-71), the Virginia-born Confederate general, was in command at Yorktown during the Peninsula Campaign in 1862, he forbade soldiers to bring liquor into the camp. One day he noticed a private named Sharpe drinking from a canteen that obviously contained something more potent than water.

Magruder, who was notorious for his fondness for anything alcoholic, ordered Sharpe to give him a taste. Taking a healthy swig, the general smiled broadly, returned the canteen and promoted the terrified soldier to the rank of corporal.

Some time later, Magruder called for another guzzle, and that time he returned the canteen with these words, "You are no longer Corporal Sharpe, sir, you are now Sergeant Sharpe." At that point the newly created sergeant realized that he would merit instant promotion as long as the booze in his canteen lasted.

Unfortunately, he had attained only the rank of lieutenant when he discovered his canteen was empty.

When Magruder next called for a drink, the disappointed Sharpe, having meanwhile scoured the camp in vain for a replenishment, could only reply, "General, my liquor has played out, and I'm sorry, for if it had held out a little longer, be damned if I wouldn't have been a brigadier general before nightfall!"

To switch from the secular to the sacred, during the early 19th century when the Baptists of Williamsburg used the celebrated brick Powder Horn as a meeting place, their pastor, the Rev. Scervant Jones, uttered a pulpit witticism that sent his congregation into gales of laughter.

On that far off hot and humid Sunday morning when Jones was in the midst of an impassioned diatribe against sin and the devil, he stopped suddenly and listened intently. Then, before resuming his attack on the evils of this world and the punishments to follow in the next, he paused, wiped his brow with a red bandana, and then explained his action.

"Brothers and sisters," he began gravely, "I trust you will pardon my interruption of the Lord's business, but I thought I heard a pack of mad dogs howling outside." Then, after a dramatic pause, he continued with a chuckle. "There is no cause for alarm, however, for I find it is only our Methodist brethren across the way praising God!"

Then there is this tale concerning a man from north of Mason and Dixon's Line who was attending a convention several years ago at the old Richmond Hotel adjoining Capitol Square in Virginia's Holy City. Becoming seriously depressed, the man climbed out on a ledge beneath the window of his room and yelled down to the pedestrians below that he intended to commit suicide.

In no time, the street was crammed with gaping spectators, one of whom cried out, "Wait, for God's sake! Don't jump! Think of your wife and children!"

"I don't have any," the man on the ledge called back.

"Well, think of your father and mother!" the other man urged.

"They're long dead!" the depressed man replied, following this with "Watch out down there, here I come!"

"Please, don't jump!" the other man continued to plead, adding desperately, "Think of Robert E. Lee!"

"Who in hell is Robert E. Lee?" the would-be suicide shot back.

"You mean you don't know who Robert E. Lee is?," the incredulous man on the sidewalk called out.

"Hell, no!" the man on the ledge answered.

At that revelation, the Good Samaritan changed his tune abruptly. Cupping his hands like a megaphone, he offered the man contemplating self-destruction one last piece of advice. "Well," he bellowed, "go ahead and jump, you Yankee SOB!"

There is also this yarn concerning General Joseph E. Johnston (1807-91), another Virginia-born Confederate general, which proves that contrary to sentimental propaganda, not every Southern youth was in the forefront of battle defending his fireside from the Yankees. One of these who weathered the war in comparative safety behind the lines was finally verbally annihilated a few years later by General Johnston.

The general was enjoying an after-dinner cigar on a Chesapeake Bay steamer when he was engaged in conversation by what was then known as a "long-range fire-eater." Waxing eloquent in his denunciation of the victorious North, the fellow wound up his tirade by declaring, "The South was not conquered, sir! She was not, nor ever will be, subdued!"

Fixing the bellicose young man with a sharp eye, Johnston asked an embarrassing question: "What was your regiment, sir?" "Unfortunately, circumstances made it impossible for me to be in the army...." the suddenly subdued fire-eater began.

"Well, I was," Johnston shot back. "And let me tell you something, young man. You may not be subdued, but I am!"

To ring down the curtain with a prime example of Virginia ecclesiastical wit, there is this story of a long-departed Episcopal bishop. Toward the end of his life the prelate was conducting a confirmation service in a church, the altar rail of which was punctuated at regular intervals with large, round oaken finials. By then, the bishop was not only old, he had also become extremely absentminded. As he moved down the line with his eyes gazing heavenward while he laid his hands on the heads of those being confirmed, he unwittingly bestowed the rite on the golden oak communion rail knobs at the same time.

Later, when he was disrobing in the vestry, the rector of the church commented, "Bishop, that was a most impressive service, but I hate to tell you that in performing your office you also extended it to the finials on the altar rail."

"Well," the bishop replied with a wry smile, "I've confirmed many a human blockhead in my time, but apparently this is the first time I've extended the rite to the real thing!"

"The Night *After* Christmas"

Almost everyone is acquainted with Clement Clarke Moore's delightful seasonal poem, "A Visit From St. Nicholas," which he wrote as a Christmas present for his children in 1822. It would be a rare individual however, who could truthfully claim to know that Dr. Robert Archer, a Norfolk-born physician and industrialist, was the author of an equally charming parody of Moore's perennial Yuletide verses.

Born in 1795, Archer was Norfolk's health officer during the early 1820s. In August 1826, he was appointed to the United States Medical Corps in which he served as an army surgeon until his retirement 25 years later. While Archer was stationed at Fort Monroe, his daughter, Sallie, married Joseph Reid Anderson, the enterprising Southern industrialist who became the owner of the Tredegar Iron Works in Richmond in 1848. After his retirement, Archer moved to Richmond, where he became a partner with his son-in-law in the Tredegar enterprise, which Civil War historians justly call the "Mother Arsenal of the Confederacy."

Archer possessed marked mechanical ability which helped Anderson to develop the Tredegar into what one writer refers to as "unquestionably the South's most important antebellum and wartime manufacturing establishment."

During Archer's affiliation with the Tredegar, which was named for an equally famous ironworks in Tredegar, Wales, the company provided the greater part of the ordnance used by the Southern armies. Notably, it also furnished the armor plate for the CSS *Virginia*, better known in history as the *Merrimack*, the famous Confederate warship that locked horns with the USS *Monitor* in the first battle between ironclads on March 9, 1862.

Even though his sympathies were with the South, Archer, like his Anderson son-in-law, realized the futility of continuing to fight after Lee had surrendered at Appomattox. After swearing allegiance to the United States, he was pardoned by President

Andrew Johnson in September 1865.

Meanwhile, Archer had sired a large family, and by the time he wrote his parody on Moore's earlier poem beginning "'Twas the night before Christmas," he had a bevy of adoring grandchildren. Remembered by his family as a sweet-tempered man and a great lover of children. Archer, at age 71, wrote his poem titled "The Night After Christmas" for his children's offspring the year after the Civil War ended. Treasured as an heirloom in verse, Archer's poem circulated only in his family until 17 years after his death in 1877, at which time permission was granted for it to be printed in The Richmond Times for December 27, 1884. It reads:

> Twas the night after Christmas, and all through the town
> The nurses were running — some up and some down.
> The doctor was wanted, for a plague on Old Nick.
> His visit had made all the little ones sick.
> His cakes were so nice, and his pies were so sweet,
> That from morning till night they did nothing but eat.
> Their hearts were all light and peeped out of their eyes;
> Their stomachs were tight and chock full of mince pies.
> They were merry as larks — had no care for tomorrow,
> Unmindful that joy is soon followed by sorrow.
> The lights were all out and the blinds were all closed;
> Papa and Mamma in deep slumber reposed.
> The cat on the hearth was licking her paws,
> And seemed to be thinking of old Santa Claus.
> The fire in the chimney burned cheerful and bright,
> And the frost on the panes shone like crystals of light.
> The teakettle, bubbling before the warm blaze,
> Was singing the dirge of once happier days.
> The clock on the mantel had just sounded one,
> And announced that another new day had begun.
> When hark! from the nursery a solo of moans,
> Then a duet of sobs, with a chorus of groans,
> Broke in on the stillness and silence of night,
> And threw the whole house in confusion and fright.
> The mother's quick ear first encountered the sound;
> She jumped up in bed and sprang out with a bound;
> But Papa had oft witnessed such tumults before,

And the louder the groans, why the louder he'd snore;
But, oh, such a scene was ne'er witnessed before —
The children were rolling about on the floor.
The bed clothes were ruined, the carpet was spoiled,
And their pretty night dresses were rumpled and soiled.
The nurse, all bewildered, was fretting and grieving;
The children, in concert, were retching and heaving.
"Oh, me, I'm so sick, I shall die of this pain;
I'll never touch Santa Claus' candy again!"
Poor Ma, in a flutter, threw up her sad eyes;
Little Bob, with a splutter, threw up his mince pies.
And Saint Nick, who was peeping, cried out with a titter;
"In everything sweet there's a drop that is bitter,
But cheer up my children, you'll soon be all right."
And cracking his whip, he soon dashed out of sight.
The crisis was over, and all went to bed.
Sweet slumber soon fell upon each dizzy head.
The life blood again freely coursed in their veins,
And dreams of Saint Nicholas danced in their brains.
With a smile they awoke from their visions of bliss,
And Mamma on each rosy lip planted a kiss.
And they vowed that in spite of all sickness and pain.
They would hang up their stockings next Christmas again.

Part 5: Just Visiting Here

The Royal Road to Virginia

Like everyone else, with the exception of a few dyed-in-the-wool Anglophobes, I followed the accounts of the visit during the Reagan era of Prince Charles and his fairy-tale princess to Washington and Palm Beach. But my interest went a step farther than that of the average person, for I had high hopes of adding a memorable anecdote or two to my file on the occasional appearance of royal birds of passage in this country.

This time, however, there were not many amusing episodes to relish, unless you care to include President Reagan's gaffe of toasting Princess Diana as "Princess David" at the White House formal dinner, or the prince's query, "Is this queen-sized or king-sized?" when he was presented with a patchwork quilt during the royal couple's visit to a shopping mall.

Of course, like any conscientious columnist, I filed these two items away among the trivia that might possibly serve later as journalistic fodder. In doing so, I rediscovered several yarns in the same folder dating from earlier American drop-ins by British and other royalty that are much more notable than the recent presidential slip of the lip or an attempt on the part of a visiting princeling to ascertain the dimensions of a hand-sewn coverlet.

For instance, take the visit of Prince Charles' great-great-grandfather, the man who later became Edward VII, to Virginia in 1860, during which he came up with a quick quip that is still regarded as one of the crown jewels of Old Dominion social history.

The prince, the eldest son of Queen Victoria and her German consort, Prince Albert of Saxe-Coburg-Gotha, was then touring Canada and the United States. When he arrived in Richmond, high society gave him the double red-carpet treatment, the climax of which was an elaborate banquet which the prince did not leave until he had consumed a great deal of champagne.

Unfortunately, the prince's schedule did not permit him time to sleep it off the next morning, and he was forced to attend St. Paul's Episcopal Church, whose rector, the Reverend Charles Minnigerode, a German, spoke with a heavy, guttural accent. All went well until the rector began his sermon, at which time the prince dozed off.

Later, while greeting members of the congregation at the church door, he was reproached by a querulous old lady for having slept throughout the sermon. But the prince was equal to the occasion, for he quickly replied, "Oh, no! Dr. Minnigerode's delightful accent made me think of my dear father, so I closed my eyes that the illusion might be perfect!"

In 1877, when the Russian Imperial Grand Duke Alexis paid Norfolk a visit and was invited to attend a ball in his honor, he inquired into the social position of those he would be expected to associate with on that occasion. When he learned that the two top leaders of Norfolk society were a grocer and an auctioneer, he is reported to have raised his eyebrows heavenward and remarked, "Really! Am I to be presented to Norfolk society by a shopkeeper and be forced to dance with the wife of the town cryer?"

Still another choice royal anecdote dates from the time Queen Elizabeth II and Prince Philip were paying their visit to Virginia in 1957 during the 350th anniversary of the first settlement at Jamestown. At a reception at the Governor's Palace in Williamsburg, a Virginia grande dame swept up to the prince and announced that she was as well-born as he, adding that she could trace her British ancestry back for 10 generations on both sides of her family.

At that point, Prince Philip cocked his head on one side, gave the matron an amused smile, and remarked dryly, "You've got it all over me, ma'am! I'm Greek!"

But my favorite royalty story is a prime example of the type of pardonable snobbery that refuses to admit that anyone — even crowned heads — is better born than the First Families of Virginia.

In November 1954, when the Queen Mother (the mother of Queen Elizabeth II) was visiting the Commonwealth, an editorial writer on the Richmond Times-Dispatch pontificated: "Virginia is particularly pleased to be on Her Majesty's itinerary, in view of the remarkable fact that she and George Washington and Robert E. Lee have a common ancestor in Colonel Augustine Warner, of Gloucester County. This means that Queen Mother Elizabeth is kin, albeit distantly, to many present-day Virginians. Some of those who will meet her in Richmond or in Williamsburg are her 'cousins,' as we say in Virginia."

George Sandys, Poet in Residence

Most literate Virginians are familiar with the quotation "A thing of beauty is a joy forever," the opening line in John Keats' "Endymion," published in 1818. Few, however, are aware of the poem's Virginia connection. The poet drew his inspiration for his retelling in rhyme of the classic story of the shepherd who loved and won the goddess of the moon from reading George Sandys' translation of Ovid's *Metamorphoses*. The earlier author largely "Englished" it from the Latin original while he lived at Jamestown from 1621 to 1631.

Keats' debt to Sandys is spelled out in detail in any number of books dealing with his poetical development and is more succinctly mentioned in *George Sandys: Poet Adventurer* (1955) by Richard Beale Davis. In summarizing Sandys' literary influence on one of the greatest English poets, Davis wrote: "Keats in the new Romantic period found in Sandys' translation many a fascinating story which he was to use in his greatest poems, including, 'Hyperion' and 'Endymion.'" Sadly, Sandys' reputation as a poet and an important founding father of the Old Dominion has so faded that he is known only to scholars of early 17th century English literature or specialists in the first years of Virginia's long history.

Born in 1578, Sandys (pronounced Sands) was the youngest son of Edwin Sandys, archbishop of York, and a brother of Sir Edwin Sandys, the English parliamentarian and major promoter of the colonization of Virginia. As the man who has been called "the morning-star at once of poetry and of scholarship in the new world," George Sandys was already a seasoned traveler and author when he embarked for Virginia in July 1621 at the age of 43.

Earlier, after studying at Oxford and the Middle Temple in London, Sandys had married Elizabeth Norton. The union had ended in a permanent separation by 1606. Four years later he embarked on an extensive ramble across Europe that took him to Venice, from which he traveled to the Near East to spend a year in Turkey, Palestine and Egypt.

This leg of his journey included a visit to the Holy Sepulcher in Jerusalem and the Pyramids of Egypt. Returning to Italy, where he tarried long enough to examine what was left of classical Rome, Sandys proceeded to England where he published an extensive account of his journey that caused a sensation.

Sandys' book, dedicated to Charles I, then Prince of Wales, was a best seller throughout the 17th century and was used as source material by Sir Francis Bacon, John Milton and other writers.

Once his travel book had been well received, Sandys began to turn his attention to the recently founded colony of Virginia. When Sir Francis Wyatt, governor and captain general of Virginia from 1621 to 1624 and husband of Sandys' niece, Margaret, sailed in 1621 for "James City in the Kingdome of Virginia," Sandys went with him as the Virginia Company treasurer.

Before departing for Virginia, Sandys had already translated the first four books of Ovid's *Metamorphoses*, the Latin narrative poem recounting legends involving miraculous transformations from the creation to the time of Julius Caesar. While en route to the new colony, Sandys versified two more books of the same work "amongst the roreing of the Seas, the rustling of the Shrouds, and the Clamour of the Saylers."

Arriving at the primitive outpost of Jamestown, Sandys was soon deeply involved in the promotion of the Virginia enterprise. Meanwhile, during his free time he finished translating the final books of the *Metamorphoses*, sending them upon completion to his publisher in England. In that way, his translation became the first serious literary work ever attempted on English American soil.

But Sandys' literary efforts did not progress without interruptions, the major one being the Indian massacre that broke like a bloody wave over the infant colony on March 22, 1622. Sandys headed a punitive expedition in the wake of the massacre, and not many months later the street singers in London were bawling a ballad which contained this verse:

Stout Master George Sandys upon a night did bravely
    venture forth
And 'mongst the Savage murtherers did forme a deede of
    worth.
For finding many by a fire to death their lives they pay
Set fire of a town of theirs and bravely came away.

During his 10 years in Virginia as company treasurer and
later as a member of the governor's council, Sandys tried to
encourage the manufacture of iron and silk in the colony, but
these efforts and his attempts to foster glass production were
foiled by the 1622 massacre and later unfavorable conditions
beyond his control. In order to obtain a superior quality of sand
for the Jamestown glasshouse, Sandys even sent a vessel to Cape
Henry for a supply from the wind-swept dunes.

But the indifference of the Italian glass blowers thwarted
his efforts and Sandys finally gave up, branding the uncooperative
workmen as "a more damned crew Hell never vomited."

Returning to England in 1631, Sandys discovered that his
translation of Ovid, which had been published in his absence, had
proved a great success. He was appointed a gentleman of the
Privy Chamber by Charles I, after which he became a leading
intellectual figure in the troubled times immediately preceding
the English Civil War. Sandys was a deeply spiritual man, and his
later poetical efforts were of a strictly religious nature.

Later in the 17th century, the poet John Dryden called
Sandys "the best versifier of the former age." Still later,
Alexander Pope declared that "English poetry owes much of its
present beauty to Sandys' translations." Keats' appreciation,
which has already been noted, came much later.

The Virginia experience had aged Sandys considerably,
however, and he finally retired to Boxley Abbey in Kent to live
with his niece, Lady Wyatt, the widow of the former Virginia
governor. In 1641, when he was 63, Sandys was described as "a
very aged man with a youthful soul in a decaying body." He died
three years later and was buried in Boxley Church near the home
that had sheltered him during the last years of his adventurous

life. Later, his relations set up a tablet in the summer house of Boxley Abbey, the large gilt letters on which proclaimed: "In this place Mr. G. Sandys, after his travails over the world, retired himself for his poetry and contemplation."

Witty as Well as Famous

It would be difficult to conjure a more unlikely foursome than President Andrew Jackson, better known as "Old Hickory"; Samuel L. Clemens, who wrote under the name Mark Twain; F. Scott Fitzgerald, the Jazz Age novelist; and Lord Louis Mountbatten, first Earl Mountbatten of Burma.

Even so, the quartet had one thing in common: Each contributed a memorable anecdote to the social history of the Norfolk area.

To begin with Jackson, on July 10, 1829, he visited what is now the Norfolk Naval Shipyard in Portsmouth to check on the progress on the first stone drydock built in the United States, begun two years earlier and completed in 1834. In the excitement kicked up by his visit, Jackson became separated from his official party, and this resulted in a delightful encounter.

Ebenezer Thompson, a Portsmouth resident who lived to be more than 90, remembered being a waterboy for the dock workmen at the time of Jackson's visit. On that eventful day, while he was eagerly pursuing his duties, he recalled, he was stopped by a tall, white-haired gentleman who asked him for a drink of water.

Seeing at a glance that the request did not come from a workman, Thompson replied: "I haven't time, sir. I'm hired by the government to wait on its employees."

"Then, my lad," the tall gentleman replied, "I am entitled to a drink for I, too, am employed by the government, as its president. Andrew Jackson at your service!"

As for Mark Twain, a case of mistaken identity was the occasion of a witty impromptu speech on his part at a reception given by the Norfolk Board of Trade on April 2, 1909. Twain was in Norfolk as the guest of his friend, Henry Huttleston Rogers, vice president of Standard Oil Company, who had just financed the completion of the Virginian Railway linking a million acres of the best coal lands in West Virginia with Hampton Roads.

At the reception in Rogers' honor, Twain stood first in the receiving line, and as many of those present apparently did not know what either he or Rogers looked like, many of them heartily congratulated Twain for having built the Virginian Railway.

After the handshaking, when cries of "Speech!" filled the hall, Twain mounted a leather-covered chair and addressed the crowd as follows:

"My friends, while I have been shaking your hands, I have listened to some very flattering compliments. I like compliments, especially those which seem to come from the heart, as yours did. They went straight to my heart, and I thank you all. I could not help but be flattered as you passed and thanked me so sincerely for the splendid road I have built through your state. I like compliments, gentlemen, and I thank you."

At that point, according to an account in The Virginia-Pilot the next day, the crowd roared.

Turning to F. Scott Fitzgerald, on one occasion after he had skyrocketed to fame for *This Side of Paradise,* he arrived by train in Norfolk to visit his first cousin, Mrs. Richard Calvert Taylor, who lived on Gosnold Avenue in the Colonial Place area.

Fitzgerald was met at Union Station on East Main Street by a rather naive young male member of the family. During the automobile drive to Taylor's house, Fitzgerald complained of being weary of the constant round of cocktail and dinner parties he was being forced to attend because of his growing celebrity as an author.

This caused the young relative to inquire, "Oh, do you write?"

"Certainly," the somewhat baffled, and possibly miffed, Fitzgerald shot back. "Haven't you read my book?"

There was a moment of silence. Then the young man replied, "Not unless you wrote *Black Beauty.*"

As for Lord Louis Mountbatten, when he visited Norfolk after World War II as First Lord of the Admiralty and one of NATO's chieftains, a group of Navy brass took him to see the cannonball embedded in the southeast corner of the altar end of historic St. Paul's Episcopal Church. With considerable relish, they pointed out that a gunner on one of Lord Dunmore's warships had fired the ball on January 1, 1776, when Virginia's last Royal Governor bombarded Norfolk in one of the British navy's less majestic episodes.

After the explanation, the American gold-braided worthies stood back and waited, presumably with inward smirks, for the celebrated sea dog's reaction.

There was a long pause while Mountbatten examined the cannonball. Then he fired a broadside of his own.

"Hahnnh," he snorted, gazing coolly at the rusty old artifact bulging from the corner of the wall. "Damn near missed it, didn't he?"

A Wilde Evening in Norfolk

The gospel of aestheticism, or art for art's sake, was proclaimed in Norfolk for the first time by Oscar Wilde (1854-1900), the self-anointed Irish-born British apostle of the "too preciously sublime" and the "too utterly utter."

Wilde's appearance on the stage of Van Wyck's Academy of Music on Main Street on the hot and humid night of July 10, 1882, was in connection with an American lecture tour sponsored by Richard D'Oyly Carte, the successful British producer of Gilbert and Sullivan's phenomenally popular "HMS Pinafore" (1878) and "The Pirates of Penzance" (1879).

When the same musical and writing team's "Patience: or Bunthorne's Bride," a satire on the then current esoteric aesthetic movement in which Wilde was caricatured, made its debut in London in 1881, D'Oyly Carte conceived the brilliant idea of sending Wilde to the United States in advance of the operetta's New York opening as a publicity stunt to acquaint the American public with the highfalutin art movement that it spoofed.

Wilde, then 27, readily accepted D'Oyly Carte's generous offer of $200 a lecture plus all expenses and embarked for the New World, cultivating a decided lisp on the way across the Atlantic which he later used to good advantage in his lectures on the decorative arts.

Arriving in New York, Wilde informed a startled customs inspector that he had nothing to declare but his genius. He then set out on an extensive lecture tour that took him to all parts of the country. His Norfolk appearance was the next to the last lap of his Southern wanderings that had included appearances in New Orleans, Atlanta, Savannah, Charleston and Wilmington, N.C., with a stopover at Beauvoir, the Mississippi estate of Jefferson Davis, in order to pay his respects to the president of the former Confederacy.

Wilde's private reaction to Davis, whom Sam Houston, the great Texan, once characterized as "ambitious as Lucifer and cold as a lizard," was expressed in a private letter to Julia Ward Howe, the author of "The Battle Hymn of the Republic." In it, Wilde quipped "how fascinating failures are," a sentiment that Mrs. Howe fortunately kept to herself.

In the main, however, Wilde was sympathetic with the Southern cause. But after his return to England he deplored the "melancholy tendency" among most of the survivors of the Late Unpleasantness, especially the elderly, "to date every event of importance by the late war."

Wilde arrived in Norfolk on the morning of July 10, 1882, and stayed at the old Atlantic Hotel on the northwest corner of Main and Granby streets, reportedly visiting Ocean View that afternoon to take advantage of the cooling sea breezes.

Meanwhile, his appearance in Norfolk had been heralded by all of the newspapers, particularly The Public Ledger, which published the following poem in the Scottish style by a local versifier named Harry Harrington on its front page on the day that Wilde arrived in the city:

> Oh, Oscar Wilde, oh, Oscar Wilde,
> You darling too too utter child,
> Why should you come sae many a mile
> Frae home to lecture?
> The love-sick maiden ye beguile
> Past all conjecture.
>
> And turn the country upside down
> As you prance on frae town to town,
> Though Billy Gilbert fuss and frown
> And name you silly,
> You care na for his gibes a crown,
> You calla lily.
>
> I'd mickle like to hear your lay
> Of things aesthetical to-day;
> I have no siler left to pay,
> And can na trick it;
> Oh! ope your British heart and say,

"Friend, here's a ticket."

Wilde's appearance on the stage of the Academy, where he held forth before a small audience of "the best class of theatre goers," was spectacular. Dressed in a black velvet "fan-tailed" coat, a long black satin vest from which dangled an enormous gold watch fob, black satin knee breeches, dark stockings, black patent leather pumps and a waterfall of lace cascading from his shirtfront and cuffs, he deplored the then-popular late Victorian Eastlake style of domestic furnishings that the whims of fashion have again skyrocketed into popularity.

Wilde left Norfolk on the morning of July 11, 1882, for Richmond, where he not only gave the same lecture he had delivered in Norfolk, but where he also delighted the devotees of the late Confederacy by climbing to the roof of the Virginia State Capitol, from which he gazed down on the Holy City of the Southland and declared that it "was worth dying for."

But that isn't the best story dating from Wilde's tour through the former Confederate states. Shortly before reaching Norfolk, he rhapsodized one evening to a matron concerning the unique beauty of Southern moonlight. There was a pause, then the loyal daughter of Dixie replied: "Yes, Mr. Wilde, it is beautiful, but you should have seen it before the war!"

Gertrude Stein, Alas

Norfolk and other parts of Virginia have interesting links with Gertrude Stein, the "rose is a rose is a rose" writer who was born in Pennsylvania in 1874 and died in Paris in 1946.

After completing her academic education, Miss Stein became an expatriate in 1903, settling in Paris, where her salon became a famous gathering place for writers, musicians and painters. At the same time she developed an incomprehensible style of writing which gained her few readers until *The Autobiography of Alice B. Toklas* was published in 1933. This book, which was really a biography of Miss Stein as seen through the eyes of Miss Toklas, her companion for most of her lifetime, became a best seller. It was followed by Miss Stein's libretto for Virgil Thompson's opera, "Four Saints in Three Acts," a 1934 theatrical bombshell that resulted in her being invited to lecture in the United States.

Before her arrival, Michael Agelasto, a Norfolk cotton broker who was prominent in the cultural life of the city for many years, sent Miss Stein a complimentary review of the opera and one of his original block prints. Pleased with Agelasto's courtesy, Miss Stein replied in typical fashion. Fortunately, when Agelasto died in 1949, his good friend, Louis I. Jaffe, then editor of The Virginian-Pilot, insisted on printing the Stein note in Agelasto's obituary. It reads:

Dear Mr. Agelasto:

Thanks so much. You do understand and I am pleased and grateful. I like your block illustration a lot. Judging from accounts the importance of the opera is beginning - as I said in composition as explanation - to make anybody see the beauty, and once they see the beauty they see nothing else. And so one does appreciate those who saw before they saw only the beauty.

Faithfully yours, Gertrude Stein

Miss Stein added the following postscript: *I used to know Norfolk, Va., but at that time it had neither apartments nor numbers 600.*

The "600" refers to Agelasto's address at that time: Hague Apartments, 606 Fairfax Ave., Norfolk.

Gertrude Stein and Miss Toklas were in this country from October 1934 to May 1935, during which time Miss Stein gave numerous lectures to audiences whose members, though they sometimes wondered what she was saying, plainly demonstrated admiration and affection.

Miss Stein was in Virginia twice during her 1934-35 tour. She spent New Year's Eve in 1934 and the next day as the stellar guest at a house party at "Westover," William Byrd's elegant 18th century James River plantation house, where her hosts, Mr. and Mrs. Richard Crane, regaled her with "spoonbread and little tenderloins of pork."

Later, in February 1935, she lectured in Charlottesville, Richmond, Williamsburg and elsewhere in Virginia. Her Richmond visit, at which time she stayed at the Jefferson Hotel and was fascinated by the "baby alligators" in the lobby pool, was a social as well as a literary success. Ellen Glasgow, the doyenne of Virginia novelists, entertained her regally at a dinner party and reception that has since become a much embroidered legend of the former capital of the Confederacy. Miss Stein's Richmond visit also was the occasion of a memorable anecdote that happened at another party.

According to the late Hunter Stagg, one of the original editors of The Reviewer, a Richmond-based literary magazine, a well-known, no longer living poetess out-Steined Stein when she was presented to the formidable Gertrude. Peering at the guest of honor through her lorgnette, the poetess declared, "Miss Stein, you amaze me!" adding, "Your picture in the paper led me to expect a vertical physiognomy, but now I find you have a horizontal one...!" At that cryptic remark, Miss Stein roared with laughter, calling out, "Alice! Alice! Come quickly! There's a wit south of the Mason and Dixon Line!"

Soon after this encounter, Miss Stein left Richmond for other parts of the country, leaving many pleasant memories behind. This euphoria, as far as diehard Confederates were concerned, was shattered two years later, however, with the publication of Miss Stein's *Everybody's Autobiography* containing an account of her American tour.

While in Richmond, Miss Stein did a good deal of walking and, being an avid Civil War buff, was amazed at the number of monumental statues to Confederate leaders that adorned the Holy City of the Southland. This caused her to meditate on the Late Unpleasantness, particularly on Robert E. Lee, whom she branded in her book as a "weak man" because "he always acted like a man leading a country in defeat."

If Miss Stein's libretto for "Four Saints in Three Acts" had been a bombshell in New York in 1934, her evaluation of Lee in *Everybody's Biography* was the equivalent of a nuclear explosion. Its publication coincided with the 1937 annual convention of the United Daughters of the Confederacy, which had chosen Richmond for that year's meeting. Needless to add, Miss Stein's disparagement of Lee, the chief saint in the Confederate hagiography, was greeted with everything from furious rebel yells to condescending appraisals by toplofty Yankee-haters who declared that she was "more to be pitied than censured."

But the best reaction came from Mrs. James L. Tyree of Richmond, who was chairman of the music committee for that year's UDC convention. As Mrs. Tyree's defense of Lee and her rationalization of what happened at Appomattox are unique, they deserve to be published in full.

"Why, General Lee was one of the strongest of men," Mrs. Tyree exclaimed. "He never surrendered, you know. He said the Confederates would lay down their arms if their implements were returned to them, so they could go back to work."

Poe in Virginia

Even though Edgar Allan Poe was a native of Massachusetts, having been born in Boston in January 1809, he considered himself a Virginian since many of the 40 years of his tragic life were intimately connected with the Old Dominion.

Poe, whom the New England poet James Russell Lowell once stigmatized as "three-fifths of him genius and two-fifths sheer fudge," was brought to Norfolk in the fall of 1810 by his actress mother, Elizabeth Arnold Poe, after she had been deserted by her husband, David Poe, an indifferent actor and a son of an Irish-born American Revolutionary War patriot.

While in Norfolk, Mrs. Poe, who was one of the most popular American actresses of her day, gave birth to a daughter, Rosalie. The child's father, according to contemporary gossip, was John Howard Payne, later the author of *Home, Sweet Home,* who was then enjoying great popularity as a juvenile theatrical star.

When Poe's mother died of tuberculosis in Richmond in December 1811, little Edgar was taken into the home of John Allan, a prosperous Scottish tobacco merchant, whose childless wife, born Frances Valentine Keeling, was a native of Princess Anne County, now the city of Virginia Beach.

In 1815, when the Allans sailed for Scotland for an extended visit, Poe and his foster parents embarked from Norfolk. Although Poe idolized Mrs. Allan, he came to despise her husband because of his philandering.

This knowledge, together with the gambling debts that Poe incurred while attending the University of Virginia, finally brought on a rupture between Allan and his foster son. As a result, Poe left Richmond when he was 18 and enlisted in the U.S. Army under the assumed name of "Edgar A. Perry." Poe's Army career, which continued until April 1829, included a tour of duty at Fort Monroe, where a special exhibit concerning his stay at Old Point Comfort is now a major attraction in the Casemate

Museum of the fort.

Toward the end of his stay at Fort Monroe, Poe's beloved foster mother died, after which her husband not only relented sufficiently to pay for a substitute to complete the rest of Poe's enlistment, but used his influence to gain Poe an appointment to the U.S. Military Academy at West Point.

Although Poe entered the academy in July 1830, his heart was not in the Army career that Allan hoped he would follow. Since by then Poe had made up his mind to be a writer, he deliberately cut classes and absented himself from drills except a final one that resulted in his expulsion. All of which serves to introduce an anecdote that reveals Poe as somewhat of a sardonic humorist.

Having decided to quit the academy, where he was irked by the stringent routine, Poe searched for a fitting way to leave a lasting impression behind him. According to an unverified but cherished West Point tradition, Poe found what he was seeking when a full dress review was ordered for January 1831. The uniform usually worn for occasions of that sort was generally the same, only the extra trappings being included in the order of the day, those for that particular occasion reading: "For the review, white cartridge belts crossed and worn under the arms."

Obeying the literalness of the instructions in order to create a sensation, Poe is reputed to have turned up for his last review wearing white cartridge belts under his arms — and nothing else. Needless to add, he was court-martialed on January 28, 1831, for "gross neglect of duty" and "disobedience of orders" and was dismissed from the academy.

Accounts of Poe's subsequent literary career, during which he became the first American writer to achieve universal fame, are readily available, but two lesser-known episodes from the Virginia chronicle of his checkered career should be mentioned. From December 1835 until January 1837, Poe was the editor of The Southern Literary Messenger in Richmond. He greatly increased the magazine's circulation but was eventually discharged for excessive drinking. Also during the same period, he married his 13-year-old cousin, Virginia Clemm, in 1836, he being 14 years older than the bride.

Later, after his wife's death in 1847, having meanwhile written many of the works by which he is now remembered, as well as having "invented the detective story," Poe returned to Richmond in 1849 to gain support for The Stylus, a literary journal he hoped to establish. During his last visit to Virginia, Poe came to Norfolk on September 8, 1849, to lecture, an event that took place on September 14 after he had spent a weekend with friends at the Hygeia Hotel at Old Point Comfort. While there, he entertained the group by reciting many of his poems on the moonlit veranda of the hotel overlooking Hampton Roads.

The details of Poe's death in Baltimore on October 7, 1849, of "congestion of the brain" brought on by excessive drinking, are too well-known to be repeated here. But there is a 20th century anecdote in which his name played an important role that I'd like to include to end this column on an upbeat note.

The Old Stone House on East Main Street in Richmond is frequently referred to as the Poe House because it contains many relics dating from the time when Poe edited The Southern Literary Messenger. This gave rise several years back to a mix-up caused by mispronunciation that has become a favorite legend of the former capital of the Confederacy.

A Yankee grande dame with a great admiration of Poe's literary works arrived by train in Richmond, where she took a taxi and demanded, "Take me to the Poe House." Without batting an eye, the driver took her on a long and circuitous drive that wound up three-quarters of an hour later in front of the Henrico County Poor House.

The ensuing attempt at elucidation on the part of the dowager is easily surmised.

Part 6: Some Virginia Grandees

'Lady Paradise'

If Lucy Ludwell Paradise, Virginia's most celebrated late 18th century eccentric, could return to Williamsburg today she would have no trouble recognizing the reconstructed Public Hospital, the first facility in British North America devoted exclusively to the treatment of the mentally ill, where she was confined for the last three years of her life.

Born in 1751 at Green Spring in James City County, Lucy was a great-granddaughter of Philip Ludwell I and a granddaughter of Philip Ludwell II, both prominent colonial officials and famous for a fiery temper that Lucy inherited. In 1766, she went to England to be with her father, the third Philip Ludwell, who had gone there for his health.

Before he died, he appointed a friend, Peter Paradise, as his executor. It was not long before Lucy had set her cap for his scholarly son, John, a brilliant linguist, fellow of the Royal Society and intimate friend of Dr. Samuel Johnson, whom James Boswell immortalized in one of the greatest of all biographies. John and Lucy were married in 1769, and their home became a rendezvous for the artistic and intellectual life of London.

Lucy was out of her element with such cultured people, for her main interests in life were dancing, card playing and gossip. During the early years of married life, however, she endured her husband's superior friends presumably because of the prestige their company gave her as a hostess. Even then, she displayed frequent attacks of the notorious Ludwell bad temper, and on one occasion, when Giuseppe Baretti, a friend of Dr. Johnson's, said something at one of her parties that displeased her, she seized a tea urn and dumped its scalding contents over his head.

Until the American Revolution, Lucy's income was derived from the rich tobacco plantations she had inherited, but when the break with England came, Virginia confiscated her property and Lucy and her husband were left with little on which to live. Both Lucy and her husband tried to remedy the situation by espousing the side of the colonies. That did little good while the war lasted, although it did furnish Dr. Johnson with an excuse for a pun when he referred to the sequestration of the Ludwell property as "Paradise's Loss."

Meanwhile, Lucy concentrated on getting a husband for her older daughter, also named Lucy, an act she accomplished with disastrous results. The husband Lucy hooked for her daughter was Count Antonio Barziza, an impecunious, fortune-hunting Venetian nobleman whom she snared by exaggerating the great wealth that would eventually return to the Paradises once the Ludwell holdings in Virginia were regained.

The count was taken in, married the daughter and took her off to Venice, where he treated her abominably. Meanwhile, Lucy placed her other daughter, Phillippa, in a London boarding school and set out with her reluctant husband for Virginia to try to regain her property.

As the attempt was unsuccessful at that time and Phillippa died during their absence, the Paradises returned to Europe, where Lucy bombarded Thomas Jefferson, then the American minister to France, with frantic appeals for help in regaining her Virginia inheritance. Finally, after having become hopelessly addicted to drink in his last years, John Paradise died in London in 1795. His irascible and debt-ridden wife remained until 1805, when Virginia friends made it possible for her to return to her native land.

From then until shortly before her death, Lucy lived in the historic Ludwell-Paradise House in Williamsburg, surrounded by the few trappings of her former opulent London life she had managed to save from her creditors. Known, and laughed at behind her back, as "Madame Paradise" or "Lady Paradise," Lucy became one of the stellar attractions of the town where she cut a wide swath for a time, and where many legends survive concerning her.

When she attended Bruton Parish Church on Sunday, she was always preceded by a turbaned slave bearing her prayer book on a velvet cushion at arm's length in front of him. Lucy also had a passion for fine clothes, and rarely did the owner of a new gown or bonnet have much chance to wear it before Lucy's turbaned factotum arrived to borrow it for his mistress. Tradition says that neither the clothes nor the bonnets were ever returned until they had lost their original purity and freshness.

Still another of Lucy's eccentricities was her coaching parties. Soon after arriving in Williamsburg, she had a large shed erected to house the coach she had brought from London. On special occasions she would summon the top matrons of the town for a "drive" which turned out to be unusual to say the least. When Lucy and her guests were seated in the carriage, a servant would roll the vehicle back and forth in the coach house until the hostess felt they had "driven" far enough, at which point the ladies would be airily dismissed.

Eventually these antics and the increasing violence of Lucy's temper caught up with her, and in 1812 it became necessary to confine her to the Public Hospital, forerunner of the Eastern Virginia State Hospital now in Dunbar. But the tragi-comedy had an amusing epilogue.

Upon Lucy's death in 1815, Viscount Fillipo Barziza, her grandson, came to Williamsburg to claim her personal property, her real property having already been taken over by two of her nieces on the strength of a law forbidding aliens from inheriting land in the Old Dominion.

When Barziza observed the loveliness of the young Williamsburg ladies who lived in the then mostly run-down houses of the town, he turned to a belle and remarked, "How can such charming houris come out of such dreadful hovels?" The belle retaliated by becoming his wife, and in the course of their married life presented him with 10 children.

After the last one, a boy, Barziza called on a Williamsburg lawyer and admitted that he had run out of names. Knowing that Barziza already had nine children, the lawyer laughed and said,

"Damn it, then, name him Decimus Ultimus," Latin for "tenth" and "last." It is good to report that the boy afflicted with such a ludicrous handle not only achieved maturity but also left Williamsburg for Texas, where he became a successful lawyer.

Having the Last Word

The solemn engraved or lithographed deathbed scenes of famous Americans that adorned the parlor walls of our Victorian ancestors have gone the way of the snows of yesteryear. Occasionally one encounters a survivor of this lugubrious art as I did recently in the private bar of a local wag. But its presence there among a collection of old burlesque theater posters dating from the Gay Nineties was more of a gag than a *memento mori.*

Even so, that particular picture, an ebony-framed depiction of the death of President Garfield, set me to thinking, and soon all sorts of long-forgotten similar representations began to surface in my memory. For instance, many households that I recall from my childhood treasured depictions of the last earthly moments of George Washington, but these always raised a question in my youthful mind of how the Father of His Country managed to put on such a stately appearance at such a time.

This difficulty continued until I encountered an explanation by Nathaniel Hawthorne many years later that solved the problem to my amused satisfaction. In commenting on the Squire of Mount Vernon, Hawthorne quipped, "He had no nakedness, but was born with his clothes on, and his hair powdered, and made a stately bow on his first entrance into the world."

Still another scene of the same sort was a representation of the last moments of Abraham Lincoln that an old Northern friend of my family proudly displayed among the relics of his Civil War days.

But this pictorial fall from Southern grace was more than compensated for by the dozens of similar depictions, all centered on the deathbeds of the heroes of Dixie, that plastered the walls of Confederate-oriented households in the same neighborhood.

With these recollections in mind, I thought it might be a good idea to set down a sampling of the last words of famous and less famous Virginians. For instance, Washington's "It is well" is indicative of the dignity of the man.

Jefferson was also in character. When he died on July 4, 1826, he asked, "Is this the Fourth?" Then the greatest Virginian of them all added, "I resign my soul to God, my daughter to my country."

Madison even injected a sparkle of wit into his last utterance by declaring, "I always talk better lying down," while General Winfield Scott, better known as "Old Fuss and Feathers" for his love of military finery, was in command to the last. "Peter," he ordered his servant, "take care of my horse."

Stonewall Jackson's "Let us cross over the river and rest under the shade of the trees" is easily the most poetic Virginia exit line of them all, while Lee, a soldier to the last, commanded, "Strike the tent," adding "Tell Hill that he must come up." But it took Woodrow Wilson to inject a 20th century ironic note. "Edith," he said, turning to his wife, "I'm a broken machine, but I'm ready."

So much for the final utterances of notable Virginians. Now for the last words of a few of the lesser known. I distinctly remember one codger, an ardent hunter, who enjoined his children, "Look after Spot (his pedigreed pointer), and try to be good to Emma (his wife)," thereby revealing his priorities.

Also, if that one isn't good enough, there is the lovely story told by Marshall W. Fishwick, a former professor of American Studies at Washington and Lee University. When Fishwick was standing at the bedside of a Virginia lady who was about to die, she whispered, "I'm not afraid. I believe I'll see Heaven. Then I'll see the three I've loved all my life. Jesus, my husband, and General Lee."

A former Hampton Roads woman who earned a lifetime reputation as a holy terror also had the distinction of providing her native area with its most memorable deathbed utterance.

Having spent her last days in a hospital in bellicose silence, she finally called a nurse to her bedside and demanded, "Am I dead yet?" When the attendant replied in the negative, the woman fixed her with a beady eye and shot back "Then, damn it, I ought to be," and fell back lifeless on the pillow. Her friends loved it, and the multiple transgressions of the deceased were readily forgiven by her victims because of her sardonic exit line.

Iron-Willed Lady Berkeley

Isn't it ironically amusing how history has a way of repeating itself? I refer specifically to the dominant role that first lady Nancy Reagan reportedly is playing in politics, a part that has a parallel in early Virginia when Lady Frances Berkeley, a strong-willed, thrice-married colonial dame, ruled the political roost in the Old Dominion for almost a quarter century.

Proud, imperious and fiercely partisan, Lady Berkeley was the sworn enemy of anyone who dared to question her own or her husband's political convictions. From the time of her first marriage at the age of 18 until her death in her middle 60s, she was in the thick of the Virginia political melee.

During the seven years of her married life with Sir William Berkeley, the royal governor, she became so powerful behind the scenes that many blamed the political blunders of her doddering husband on her none-too-subtle tugging at the governmental reins.

Lady Berkeley came from an English family accustomed to command. Her great-great-grandfather, Walter Culpeper (c. 1475-1516), was Under Marshal of Calais. And her haughty cousin, Thomas, Lord Culpeper, was one of Virginia's less distinguished colonial governors during the latter part of her life.

A daughter of Thomas and Katherine Culpeper, Lady Berkeley was baptized in Hollingbourne Church, Kent, on May 27, 1634. Her father lost most of his property in the British Civil War, and after the execution of Charles I, he emigrated to Virginia with his entire family.

When Frances Culpeper was 18, she married Samuel Stephens of Balthorpe plantation in Warwick County and one of the early governors of Carolina and became a behind-the-scenes political power. A few months after Stephens' death in 1670, she became the wife of Sir William Berkeley at Green Spring plantation in James City County. The bridegroom was 26 years older than the bride, and his estate, the finest in the colony, became a hotbed of intrigue under Lady Berkeley's dominance.

Bacon's Rebellion was brewing, and the governor's political policy did nothing to forestall the storm. When it broke, Berkeley sent his wife to England for her protection — and also to solicit aid against Bacon's forces, which for a while carried everything before them.

Returning to Virginia after the rebellion had been put down, Lady Berkeley became the leading light of the "Green Spring Faction." Wholesale hangings and confiscations of "rebel" property followed, much of which she aided and abetted.

This ceased only when Berkeley was ordered to England by Charles II in 1677. The king's reputed remark, "That old fool has hanged more men in that naked country than I did for the death of my father," became the unofficial epitaph of the embittered old governor.

At the height of the bickering between the Royal Commissioners and the Berkeley faction, Lady Berkeley perpetrated a spiteful insult that Philip Alexander Bruce in his *Institutional History of Virginia in the Seventeenth Century* describes as follows:

The Commissioners sent out to Virginia to inquire into the causes of the insurrection of the previous year had called at Green Spring, the home of Sir William Berkeley, whose bitter enmity they had incurred by their condemnation of his violent conduct in punishing the unfortunate followers of Bacon. When they left the house, the Governor's coach was waiting at the door ready to convey them to Jamestown. Apparently they were to be the recipients of an attention worthy of their rank; after taking their seats within the vehicle, however, they observed to their indignant horror their postilion was the common hangman. As they drove away, they saw Lady Berkeley peeping at them in evident derision through a broken quarrel of glass in the window of her chamber.

After Sir William's death, Lady Berkeley married Colonel Philip Ludwell of Rich Neck plantation, the leader, with Lady Frances' help, of a powerful colonial upper-crust clique that furthered its own ends by baiting royal authority, veiling its actions under the hypocritical pose of championing the rights of the common people, whom they despised.

Even though she married Ludwell, Lady Berkeley never relinquished her title and was known as Lady Frances Berkeley until her death in the 1690s. She was buried in the churchyard at Jamestown, where a fragment of her tombstone can still be seen, a memento of a dangerous, iron-willed woman who left her mark on the Virginia of her time.

George Washington's Mules

Although George Washington had nothing to do with his post-mortem canonization as the Father of Our Country, he was proud to acknowledge during his lifetime that he was the earliest American sponsor of that long-eared, cantankerous critter, the mule.

By his own admission, according to Paul Leland Haworth's *George Washington, Country Gentleman*, the master of Mount Vernon was the first American to successfully breed mules, all of which chalks up another little-known priority for the Old Dominion.

Before going into Washington's angle of the story, however, it might be wise to say something concerning the mule itself.

Technically speaking, a mule is the sterile offspring of a female horse and a jackass, and the history of the species can be traced back at least 3,000 years. To cite two historical examples, mules were used as draft and farming animals in Homeric Greece, while in ancient Israel they were known before the reign of King David.

Despite the animals' longstanding popularity in southern Europe, there were no mules in colonial America, the heavy farm work having been done by horses or oxen until after the Revolutionary War. All of which serves to introduce Washington's role in making the mule a popular, if sometimes recalcitrant, American domestic animal.

According to the recollections of George Washington Parke Custis, Washington's adopted step-grandson, the master of Mount Vernon did not turn his attention to mule breeding until the 1780s. At that time he wrote the American representative in Spain to ascertain whether it would be possible "to procure permission to extract a Jack ass of the best breed" to be sent to him at Mount Vernon.

The exportation of jackasses was then forbidden by Spanish law, but the Spanish minister of state, learning of Washington's request, brought the matter to the attention of his monarch, Charles III. Wishing to honor the victor of Yorktown, the king graciously granted the request and dispatched two jackasses to the master of Mount Vernon.

One of them died en route, but the other, which was named Royal Gift and later served as a subject of Washington's ribaldry, arrived on December 5, 1785. Later, Lafayette presented his old companion in arms with another jackass from the island of Malta, which was immediately dubbed Knight of Malta.

Unlike Royal Gift, which at first declined to mate with the mares in the Mount Vernon pastures, Knight of Malta, who was described as "having the form of a stag and the ferocity of a tiger," was ready for business at hand. Not to be outdone, Royal Gift finally emulated Knight of Malta's procreative activities, the result being that the mules they sired became the forerunners of the animals that were used for years for draft purposes by the U.S. Army as well as those employed as farm animals throughout the South before they were outmoded by automotive tractors and cultivators.

Meanwhile, the mule became part and parcel of Southern folk speech and folklore. For instance, a pushy or unduly aggressive person is still frequently referred to by Southerns as "having the nerve of a government mule." And who of us (the readers and the author of this column excepted, of course) haven't known people who were "as stubborn as a mule?"

Also, throughout the Southland, many unpleasant situations are still referred to as being "enough to make a mule leave his oats," while one anonymous Dixie misogynist went so far as to declare: "The female of the species is more dangerous than the mule."

Even William Faulkner, who eulogized the mule at great length in *Sartoris,* declared that the critter "will labor ten years willingly and patiently for you for the pleasure of kicking you once," while, there is also a good old Virginia yarn that presents the mule in a more sympathetic light.

The tale was set in a country camp meeting where the sweet-voiced singer who usually "raised the hymn" was absent, and his place had been taken by another worshiper with a voice like a foghorn.

After a few verses the singer noticed that a pious sister seated in front of him was sobbing uncontrollably. Fearing that she had been taken ill, he ceased singing and asked if there was anything he could do for her.

"No, thanks," she replied, "I just couldn't help breaking down. I've had such bad luck lately. I lost my husband a month ago, and a week ago my wayward son ran away. And only yesterday my old mule, Jenny, that I set such a store on, up and died."

Then, after drying her eyes, she added, "Poor thing, she used to come up to the yard gate every morning and wake me up with her braying. And when you started to sing 'Almost Persuaded,' your voice sounded so much like that poor old critter, I just couldn't hold it in any longer."

Dark Horse Harry

Even though Stratford Hall in Westmoreland County, the ancestral home of the Lees of Virginia and the birthplace of Robert E. Lee, is a stellar attraction to tourists, it is not likely that its hostesses will voluntarily tell visitors why Lee's older half-brother, Henry Lee, was forced to sell the massive brick plantation house beside the Potomac.

Henry Lee, known in the annals of Virginia scandal as "Dark Horse Harry" or "Black Horse Harry," was a quixotic and tragic character. It is therefore a great wonder, considering the prominence of his family and the events involving his downfall, that he has not been featured as the hero of a modern Gothic novel using a historical Southern background.

Detailed accounts of the affair are readily available in *Stratford Hall: the Great House of the Lees* by Ethel Ames (1936); *A Visit to Stratford and the Story of the Lees* by Alonzo T. Dill, a former reporter for The Virginian-Pilot, and Mary Tyler Cheek (1980), published by the Robert E. Lee Foundation Inc., the present owners of Stratford; *Robert E. Lee: A Portrait (1807-1861)* by Margaret Sanborn (1966); and *Lee* by Clifford Dowdey (1965). Briefly, this is the story.

Although he was not physically handsome like his illustrious half-brother, Robert E. Lee, who was almost 20 years his junior, Henry Lee was remembered by many contemporaries as a brilliant conversationalist and a man of great charm. Born in 1787 at Stratford, Lee was the only surviving son of General Henry ("Light Horse Harry") Lee, one of Washington's favorite officers, and his first wife (and second cousin), Matilda Lee. She was the heiress of Stratford from whom her son Henry inherited the estate at his majority. Robert E. Lee was a son of his father's second wife, born Ann Hill Carter of Shirley plantation in Charles City County.

After attending Washington College (now Washington and

Lee University) and the College of William and Mary, Henry Lee was elected to the Virginia House of Delegates. He also served with the American Army on the Canadian border during the War of 1812. Meanwhile, he had become the master of Stratford, where he enjoyed sharing the field sports and deer hunts with his half-brothers, notably the boy who was later to become the idol of the Confederacy.

Lee had also begun his courtship of Anne Robinson McCarty, 11 years his junior. She and her sister, Elizabeth, who was 14 years younger than Lee, and who later played a stellar role in the well-publicized scandal having Stratford as its background, were the orphans and heiresses of Daniel McCarty of Pope's Creek, a nearby plantation.

Lee and Anne McCarty were married in 1817, and a good deal of the bride's money was used to refurbish Stratford. Shortly after the marriage, the Lees persuaded Elizabeth McCarty to come and live at Stratford. Soon after her arrival she made arrangements for Harry Lee to act as her guardian in place of Richard Stuart, her mother's second husband.

Neither Lee, his wife nor his ward had any idea of economy. As a consequence, a steady depletion of the McCarty money resulted in financial troubles. Meanwhile, Anne Lee had given birth to a daughter. Two years later when the child was playing in the Great Hall at Stratford she ran out of the front door, fell down the high flight of steps leading to the yard, and was killed instantly. Anne Lee was so overcome by the tragedy that she began taking heavy doses of morphine, eventually becoming an addict.

At that point, gloom settled over Stratford, and during the ensuing months Henry Lee and his wife's younger sister Elizabeth were thrown, to use his own words, "into a state of the most unguarded intimacy." As a result, Elizabeth McCarty bore Henry Lee a stillborn child. Despite efforts to keep the matter quiet, it leaked out and Lee was branded throughout Virginia as the perpetrator of a "crime of the blackest dye," which, in view of his role as the guardian of his minor ward, intensified the situation.

As a consequence, the epithets "Black Horse Harry" and "Dark Horse Harry" were quickly applied to him. But Lee was not completely friendless, for his half-brother Charles Carter Lee went on record as saying he "did not believe that because a man did one thing wrong he was as black as Satan." Even so, Elizabeth McCarty's stepfather hastened to Stratford and took her home with him. Once she was under his roof again, Elizabeth McCarty petitioned the court to dismiss Henry Lee as her guardian and to reappoint her stepfather in his place. This action resulted in a prolonged legal battle which Stuart finally won. Before that happened, Elizabeth McCarty cut off her beautiful hair, put on deep mourning and from that time on went out in public only to church, and then heavily veiled.

From then on Lee became increasingly desperate with a morphine-addicted wife to care for and little money for day-to-day expenses. Finally, he sold Stratford in 1821 to William Clarke Somerville of St. Mary's County, Md., for $25,000. Two years after Somerville's death in 1826, Stratford was sold at auction for $11,000 to Henry D. Storke of Westmoreland County. In the meantime, Storke had married Elizabeth McCarty, Henry Lee's sister-in-law and former ward, who not only survived her husband but, ironically, became the mistress of Stratford for the next 50 years.

Lee's subsequent history can be quickly told. Although his wife left him after he sold Stratford, she was later reconciled to him through the good offices of his staunch friend, Andrew Jackson, who stood by Lee despite the persecution he continued to suffer.

Lee, who subsequently joined the Jacksonian party, aided in preparing Jackson's inaugural address in 1829. In appreciation, Jackson appointed him consul general to the Barbary States. Lee set out somewhat prematurely for Algiers. Soon after his arrival he learned that his appointment had not been confirmed by the Senate, which left him adrift in the Old World. Fortunately, his loyal half-brother, Charles Carter Lee, sent him small sums from time to time. This enabled Lee and his wife to spend the better part of 1830 in Italy, where he became a good friend of Napoleon's mother, then living in Rome.

Later, Lee and his wife settled in Paris, where he began writing a biography of Napoleon. This resulted in the publication of only the first volume, bringing his subject's career down to his first Italian campaign. Unfortunately, before the second volume was completed, Lee died of influenza in Paris in 1837. His widow survived him for three years, dying in Passy, a suburb of Paris. Both she and her husband are buried in the Parisian cemetery of Pere-Lachaise.

Martha's First Husband

George Washington in 1759 married one of the wealthiest widows in the Old Dominion. Less publicized, however, is the intriguing story — with an O. Henry twist at the end — of how Martha Dandridge Washington (1731-1802) achieved her enviable and lucrative position.

The details of the complicated events leading up to Martha's first marriage, to Daniel Parke Custis (1711-57), a man 20 years older than herself, can be found in volume two of Douglas Southall Freeman's monumental biography of Washington. Briefly, this was the scenario of the matrimonial comedy, much of which reads like an 18th century farce.

Martha's first spouse was the only son to reach maturity of an eccentric old Virginia aristocrat, Colonel John Custis III (1679-1749) of Arlington plantation on the Virginia Eastern Shore and Williamsburg, and his equally erratic wife, Frances Parke Custis, a daughter of Colonel Daniel Parke, one of Virginia's more spectacular early rakehells.

Unlike his mule-headed and hot-tempered parents, however, Daniel Parke Custis was likable and even-tempered. Even so, he had been so completely cowed by his cantankerous father that he was still a bachelor at 37, almost unheard of in the Virginia of his time, when he began courting Martha Dandridge of New Kent County.

Before that, the younger Custis had solicited any number of eligible young Virginia ladies as prospective brides. But each time a match seemed assured, his father had raised some last-minute objection, and the affair had terminated abruptly. One of Daniel's inamoratas had been a daughter of Colonel William Byrd II of Westover, whose recently discovered and published diaries reveal him to have been one of the hitherto unsuspected Virginia Casanovas of his time. But the elder Custis had been so evasive in making the arrangements for the marriage settlement that the amorous master of Westover finally dismissed young Custis by airily remarking that the Byrds could not trust to "such a phantom as Colonel Custis' generosity."

Shortly after this rebuff, Daniel met 18-year-old Martha Dandridge and made tentative overtures to gain his father's approval of the match. Fearful that the old colonel would again balk at the idea of his marrying, the younger Custis sent two of his friends, John Blair and Thomas Lee, both famous Virginians of their time, to plead his suit. Their intercession irked the colonel on two counts. First, he felt his son should have applied for his permission in person, and second, he considered the prospective bride's family inferior to his own. But that time Daniel Parke Custis did not accept his father's mandate as final, and he dispatched another matchmaker, his attorney, James Power, to see if his father would reconsider.

It so happened that a small mulatto boy named Jackie, for whom the elder Custis had developed an inordinate fancy, practically dominated the colonel's household. As Power was well acquainted with the old fellow's doting partiality for the boy, who backstair Virginia gossip avers was the colonel's wrong-side-of-the-blanket son, he used the unsuspecting boy as a pawn in the matrimonial game.

Jackie, a son of a slave of Colonel Custis' named Alice, had been freed by his master, and Power was a good enough psychologist to realize that any act of kindness or deference to the little mulatto on his part could easily be used to further his client's cause.

Unlike Blair and Lee, who preceded him and whom the colonel had summarily dismissed, Power found the crotchety old colonel in a receptive mood, as far as his son's marrying Martha Dandridge was concerned. In fact, he informed the somewhat surprised Power that he would rather have Daniel marry Martha than any other young lady in Virginia, offering this reason for his change of heart: "Her character...enamoured him as much as her person attracted Daniel." This, Custis explained, "was because of a prudent speech she had made."

Added to this revelation, when the colonel invited Power to spend the night, an invitation he rarely extended to anyone, the sharp-witted lawyer had every reason to feel that he was not on a fool's errand.

Power had ridden his young son's handsome horse from New Kent County to Williamsburg to call on the elder Custis, and when little Jackie admired the spirited steed, Power played his trump card and presented the old colonel's favorite with the horse, its saddle and bridle.

History has not recorded what Power's undoubtedly flabbergasted son said when he learned that his horse and its equippage had been used as an ace in the matrimonial game. But it is explicit in stating that his father's act of generosity so pleased old Colonel Custis that he freely gave his consent for his long-suffering son to marry the young lady of his choice.

Fortunately, Power's note to Daniel Parke Custis, scribbled hastily in Williamsburg after the colonel's assent was given, has been preserved in the Custis family papers. Addressed to the anxiously waiting younger Custis at his plantation, White House on the Pamunkey River, it reads: "Hurry down immediately (for fear) your father should change the strong inclination he has to your marrying directly."

Daniel Parke, Colonial Scamp

Two Virginians, one famous, the other infamous, participated in the Battle of Blenheim in 1704, the turning point of the War of the Spanish Succession, which was fought in West Bavaria on the Danube River.

The first was Alexander Spotswood, Virginia's Scottish-born lieutenant governor from 1710 to 1722. The second was Colonel Daniel Parke, the Old Dominion's most celebrated colonial libertine. Spotswood, serving as a colonel, was wounded at Blenheim, where the British and Austrian forces under the Duke of Marlborough and Prince Eugene of Savoy defeated the French and Bavarian armies under Marshal Tallard, ending Louis XIV's efforts to make France the dominating European power.

Spotswood's record as one of Virginia's ablest early executives is too well known to be repeated. Rather, it is Parke, the colony's most flamboyant rakehell of his time, who is of interest here.

The pampered only son of Daniel Parke Sr., treasurer and secretary of the Virginia colony, and Rebecca Evelyn, a cousin of the English diarist John Evelyn, Parke did not appear on the Virginia scene until after his father's death in 1679, when he came from England as a boy of 10 to claim his inheritance. As the conditions under which he was to inherit his father's holdings hinged on either waiting to attain his majority or marrying and taking control, Parke, after dallying for a short time, opted for the latter. His bride was Jane Cottington Ludwell, the daughter of the politically powerful Philip Ludwell I of Green Spring plantation.

Both Parke and his bride were adolescents at the time of their marriage, and although their two daughters, both of whom turned out as wilful as their father, lived to become ancestresses of many famous Virginians, their parents' marriage was disastrous.

Parke's charm gained him the patronage of Sir Edmund

Andros, one of Virginia's most unpopular royal governors. Andros loaded his youthful protege with honors, even making him a member of the Governor's Council when he was 23. Andros also used Parke as a tool against his enemy, Sir Francis Nicholson, then governor of Maryland but later lieutenant governor of Virginia, and the early records contain many examples of Parke's brutal behavior toward Nicholson.

During the same period Parke went to England. When he returned he brought back a mistress, whom he flaunted openly and by whom he had a son, Julius Caesar Parke, even though he already had a wife and two daughters living in the colony. Meanwhile, Parke had run afoul of the Reverend James Blair, the all-powerful commissary of the Bishop of London and the founder and first president of the College of William and Mary in Williamsburg, and Blair's surviving letters have preserved Parke's highhandedness for posterity like a fly in amber.

Writing to a correspondent in England, Blair commented: "There is a handsome young man of the Country (i.e., Virginia), one Mr. Daniel Parke, who to all the other accomplishments that make a complete sparkish gentleman, has added one upon which he infinitely values himself, that is, a quick resentment of every least thing that looks like an affront or injury. He has learned they say the art of fencing and is as ready at giving a challenge especially before Company, as the greatest Hector in Towne."

Blair's unfavorable opinion of Parke was not long in getting back to him and although the commissary's clerical position prevented Parke from challenging him to a duel, the sparkish colonel took another way of displaying his fury. Parke was a vestryman of Bruton Parish Church in Williamsburg but had ceased attending services because the minister had preached several pointed sermons against adultery. These were specifically aimed at Parke, who according to Blair, "at this time, and still, doth entertain a Gentleman's Lady, one Mistress Berry, whom he conveyed away from her husband in London, in 1692, and carried her to Virginia along with him, calling her by the name of his cousin Brown."

To even the score with Blair, Parke struck a blow at the latter's wife, who was seated on the Sunday the incident occurred in a pew in Bruton Parish Church belonging to Parke's father-in-law, Colonel Ludwell. In commenting on the reasons for Parke absenting himself from church and his subsequent scandalous conduct, Blair wrote:

"But to have a blow at Mr. Blair, he resolved one day to lay aside his reluctance and come to church to pull Mistress Blair out of that pew, which for that time he was pleased to claim as his own. Accordingly about the month of January 1696 he came one Sunday suddenly to Church & rushing in with great fury and mighty violence he seized Mistress Blair by the wrist and with great fury and violence pulled her out of the pew in the presence of the minister and Congregation, who had begun divine service, all the people being extremely scandalized at this ruffianly & profane action."

This affront, and the fact that Parke later committed some unspecified crime at the gaming tables in New York, made it advisable for him to leave the colonies to escape punishment. Arriving in England in 1702, he purchased an estate and was elected to Parliament. Not long afterward, however, he was expelled from the House of Commons for bribery.

In the meantime, Parke had formed a liaison with the wife of the captain of the Guards, and to escape the latter's vengeance he fled to Holland, where he joined the British military forces under the Duke of Marlborough, eventually becoming the latter's aide-de-camp.

After the Battle of Blenheim, the duke hastily scribbled a note to his wife on the back of a tavern bill announcing his victory. This was entrusted to Parke, who delivered it 10 days later to the duchess in London. She, in turn, sent Parke with the message to Queen Anne, whom Parke found playing dominoes in a window bay at Windsor Castle. As it was customary to give the bearer of victorious tidings a gratuity of 500 pounds, the queen offered this to Parke, but he begged a miniature of the queen instead. This was sent to him later with an additional gift of 1,000 guineas.

Patronized by Marlborough, Parke was appointed governor of the Leeward Islands in 1706, where his continued arrogance and his subsequent debauching of the wife of a prominent planter resulted in the bloody insurrection in which Parke, then 41, was brutally murdered on December 7, 1710.

Verses Etched in Acid

Virginians with a keen sense of humor have been scribbling light verse since the late 17th century. For instance, when Richard Cole of Westmoreland County, a gay blade in the original sense of the word, sat down in 1663 to write his will, he included this clause:

"It is my Will and Desire that my body be interred upon Poynt Pleasant uppon my plantation where I now live in a neat Coffin of Black walnutt if conveniently to be had and that a Grave Stone of Black Marble be with all convenient Speed sent for out of England, with my Coate of Armour engraved in brasse, and under it this Epitaph:

"Here lies Dick Cole a grievous Sinner
That died a little before Dinner
Yet hopes in Heaven to find a place
To satiate his Soule with Grace."

Whether Dick Cole's tombstone with its whimsical epitaph ever arrived from England is unknown, for no trace of it has ever been found at Point Pleasant in Westmoreland County. Even so, the altar tomb that memorializes Robert Carter of Corotoman, an ancestor of Robert E. Lee and countless other Virginians, was not long in acquiring an extra inscription after it had been installed over Carter's grave.

One of Virginia's most prominent early 18th century grandees, Carter was known as "King" Carter because of his imperiousness. When he died, an unknown versifier chalked the following satirical verse on his ornate tombstone in Christ Church graveyard in Lancaster County after its arrival from England:

> Here lies Robin, but not Robin Hood,
> Here lies Robin that never was good,
> Here lies Robin that God has forsaken,
> Here lies Robin the Devil has taken.

With the establishment of the Virginia Gazette in 1736, its editor, William Parks, spiced up its pages with borderline bawdy verses, a policy his successors continued. For instance, in 1775, this poem, which has a definitely modern slant, appeared in a column devoted to wit and ribaldry:

> Says Allen to his wife, before we part
> I have some serious matter much at heart.
> When I was young I was prodigious wild,
> I fell in love and got a maid with child;
> The babe is handsome, though she's rather brown;
> Do take her home, and rear her as your own.
> I wish indeed you'd her example be;
> I'm sure you'll love her, for she's much like me!
> 'Tis well my dear, and you confess in time,
> I'm glad to find by you — that it's no crime.
> I had a boy before I married you,
> Therefore together let us wed the two.

Continuing in the same earthy vein, the Winchester Mercury published this rhyming advertisement in 1788:

> I am an old man, my case is quite common,
> I want me a wife, a likely young woman.
> I late had an old one, but three months ago,
> She sicken'd and died, and left me in woe;
> I whin'd, had a sermon preach'd when she was buried.
> Wore my old wig a fortnight, then long'd to be married.
> If any one knows where a wife's to be had,
> Such as seventy wishes when reason is dead;
> A girl that will warm my old bones in the winter,
> Let them leave the intelligence with Mr. Printer.

Also along the same line is this gem from the Norfolk and Portsmouth Herald for February 19, 1812:

Tho' marriage by some folks be reckon'd a curse,
Three wives did I marry for better or worse:
The first for her person — the next for her purse
And the third for a warming pan, doctress and nurse.

There is also this well-authenticated exchange of light verse in which John Page, governor of Virginia from 1802 to 1805, was one of the principals. Toward the end of his life, Page became quite smitten with a young woman whom he met at an Alexandria dancing assembly. In the course of the evening the object of his admiration dropped one of her gloves, which Page picked up and put in his pocket. The next day he sent the glove to its owner with the following couplet:

If you from Glove to take the letter G,
The glove is Love, and that I send to thee.

John Page

To this, the young woman immediately returned this reply:

If you from Page do take the letter P,
The Page is Age, and that won't do for me.

Finally, here is a bit of Virginia folklore in verse which was imparted to me recently by my neighbor and contemporary, Allan C. Otey, a man held in the highest esteem by those who know him because of his constant efforts to keep Norfolk's West Bute Street area spick and span.

A native of Roanoke, Otey learned the delightful bit of doggerel in his youth while swimming in the buff with other boys at a place called Deep Hole on the Roanoke River. According to Otey, a constant tug-of-war went on at the swimming hole between the devil-may-care boys and the female Comstocks who surreptitiously enjoyed watching the naked swimmers until they were detected in the act. After that the prudes showed their lack of appreciation by calling the police.

Unfortunately, Otey's repertory does not include any rhymes on the nude-swimming episodes, but the one that he did learn at Deep Hole would have delighted Mark Twain's heart. Read it and be thankful that light verse is still alive and well in the Old Dominion.

> Here's to old Eve, the mother of our race,
> Who wore a great big fig leaf right in the proper place.
> Here's to old Adam, the father of us all —
> Who was Johnny on the spot when the leaves began to
>   fall!

Part 7: The Late Unpleasantness

"Dixie" Meets a Maestro

Arturo Toscanini, the late, celebrated Italian symphonic maestro, conducted a musical blockbuster in the Mosque Theater in Richmond on April 19, 1950, that resurrected the rebel spirit of the former capital of the Confederacy with a vengeance. The occasion was the second of two Richmond concerts by the 83-year-old conductor and the National Broadcasting Company Symphony Orchestra, then on a tour of 20 cities.

Toscanini had arrived in Richmond the day before the concert and was treated to a tour of many of the shrines held sacred by unreconstructed Southerners. It was during his perambulations in the footsteps of Jeff Davis and Marse Robert that he decided to heed a suggestion of his 20-year-old grandson, Walfredo Toscanini, a Yale University student. Walfredo had tried to interest him in the snappy tunes of Daniel Decatur Emmett, whose "Dixie" had been elevated from a walk-around tune he wrote in 1859 for Bryant's Minstrels to the *Gloria in Excelsis* of the Lost Cause.

In true cloak-and-dagger style that would have done justice to his Italian Renaissance ancestors, Toscanini secretly tried out one orchestral setting of "Dixie" after another on the day of the concert until he finally settled on one by Dr. Frank Black, NBC's general musical director, as the most stirring.

That night, more than 5,000 elegantly turned-out music

lovers occupied seats in the Mosque, Richmond's concert hall, not suspecting that the Italian wizard with the baton was about to give the musical cue for the South to rise again.

When Toscanini shuffled onto the podium, the dignified audience arose as one to pay him tribute. From then on, the program proceeded in a normal fashion while the maestro put his well-trained musicians through their paces in selections from Tchaikosky, Kabalevsky, Brahms, Mendelssohn and Ravel. When it was over, the audience gave the maestro another standing ovation, then settled back for the customary encore, little dreaming what a musical surprise was on the way.

They got one all right! Toscanini climbed back on the podium, raised his magic baton, and the orchestra broke into a rip-roaring rendition of "Dixie." In a moment, all hell broke loose. Staid dowagers and their proper escorts dropped their programs and opera glasses and leaped to their feet in a deafening chorus of rebel yells.

Ardent devotees of The Late Unpleasantness wept openly, while one portly matron, who looked like a one-woman embodiment of the United Daughters of the Confederacy, reached into her reticule and produced a miniature Stars and Bars, which she waved triumphantly over the heads of the wildly cheering crowd.

When it was over, the maestro, who had maintained a dignified austerity all evening, turned to the audience and grinned back at the sea of radiant faces on the other side of the footlights as he made bow after bow. But that was not the climax of the evening.

As the excited throng milled back out onto Monroe Park, one female Richmond Yankee-hater was heard to crow: "What superb timing! Why I feel so pepped up, I'm ready to hop into my cyar and head for Manassas to start the war all over again!"

War's Lighter Moments

That the Muse of Comedy has the saving grace of intervening in even the most trying situations is exemplified by the following anecdotes, all dating from the years when the South was torn asunder by what some unreconstructed Virginians still refer to as the War for Southern Independence.

The first tale dates from McClellan's Peninsular Campaign and reveals how sheer effrontery got a tired and hungry soldier a free meal in the company of his general. On the march back up the Virginia Peninsula after the Battle of Williamsburg in May 1862, Confederate General John B. Magruder and his staff visited a widow who had agreed to serve them dinner. Shortly afterward, a footsore Southern soldier knocked on the widow's back door and asked if she would give him a bite to eat.

"Why, yes," she replied, "but as I'm getting dinner now for General Magruder and his staff and haven't room at my table for more, you'll have to wait until they're through eating."

The soldier thanked her but lingered in the hall, keeping an eye on the dining room. After the servants had put the meal on the table and the widow had gone into the parlor to summon her guests, he walked in and seated himself. When the officers entered and found chairs for all but one available, the odd officer returned to the parlor to wait. General Magruder took his seat next to the soldier, and after he had finished his soup, he turned and asked if he had any idea with whom he was dining.

"Well, no, I can't say that I do," the soldier replied with a grin. "You see, I used to be kinda particular on that score, but since I started soldiering I've gotten so I don't give a damn who I eat with as long as the victuals are clean."

Magruder was so delighted with the soldier's answer that he not only overlooked his brazenness but paid for his meal besides.

The second yarn concerns a Yankee colonel who asked his hostess if he and some of his fellow officers could share her private devotions. The matron lived in a large house on Williamsburg's Palace Green, and when the federal forces occupied the town in 1862, the colonel and some of his friends were billeted in her spare rooms.

Learning that his hostess held family prayers for her household every Sunday evening, the colonel requested that he and his companions in arms might be permitted to attend. The petition was granted, and when the next Sunday rolled around the slicked-up Yankees filed up the stairs and ranged themselves around the matron's bedroom wall.

They found her seated in a comfortable chair with the Bible open on her lap while her family and servants knelt around her. Clearing her throat, the matron began. She had not gone on long, however, before the boys in blue realized they had let themselves in for a verbal bombardment. For instead of the awe-inspiring sacred selections they had expected to hear, they were treated to a stentorian reading of the most belligerent psalms in the book.

When that was over, the matron handed the Bible to a servant and knelt on the floor beside her chair. Clasping her hands, she prayed fervently for the collapse of the Union from President Lincoln on down. Tradition says a violent storm was raging outside, and the lightning and thunder, combined with the matron's hellfire and damnation, discouraged the Yankees from ever asking to share her devotions again.

The third tale recounts how a Mrs. Sully, another Williamsburg grande dame, managed to turn the tables on the occupation forces. Mrs. Sully's former home and the historic St. George Tucker House stand side by side on Nicholson Street east of Palace Green.

One afternoon during the federal occupation of the town, one of the Tucker girls looked out of a window and saw Mrs. Sully in her garden.

"You'd better keep a sharp eye on Captain Bolling, ma'am," she called out. "I saw him strutting around your garden yesterday in broad daylight, and if he's not more careful the Yankees will be sure to nab him."

The next morning Mrs. Sully's breakfast was interrupted

by a knock on her front door. Answering the summons, she was confronted by a lieutenant in blue who told her she must accompany him immediately to the provost marshal's headquarters.

When they arrived, Mrs. Sully was informed that she was known to be harboring a Confederate captain named Bolling, the Tucker girl's overheard conversation being quoted as evidence. Mrs. Sully was then told that unless she turned the officer in immediately she would be dealt with severely.

To this she made no reply except to assure the provost marshal that she would be happy to cooperate.

Returning home under guard, Mrs. Sully requested the soldiers to join her on her back porch. She took some cracked corn from a shelf and began tossing it into the yard.

"Here, chicky, chick, chick!" she called out loudly, to the soldiers' dismay. That brought her poultry running on the double. When they were all gobbling the unexpected treat, she turned to the baffled federals.

Pointing to her finest rooster, she informed them his name was General Lee. Singling out another rooster, she introduced him as General Magruder.

Then indicating a scrawny frying-sized specimen among the busily pecking chickens, she said: "Now that one, gentlemen, is Captain Bolling. He's a right smart runner, but if you ever catch him, you'll be more than welcome to him."

How Lincoln Took Norfolk

When I attended Maury High School in the 1920s, there was a humorless, pince-nez-wearing English teacher there whose Southern chauvinism was so ingrained that she solemnly warned her classes at the beginning of each semester: "Any paper on the writings of Abraham Lincoln will not be acceptable for credit in this course."

Under the pressure of such unreconstructed inflexibility, I, as a grandson of a man who had fought on the winning side, decided that compliance was the best policy. But that did not dampen my interest in the Great Emancipator. Moreover, as I learned more about local history, I was delighted to discover that the man familiarly known as Honest Abe had visited the Norfolk area on two well-authenticated occasions during the four bloody years of the Civil War.

Lincoln's initial visit took place in May 1862, when he set foot for the only time on territory now within the corporate limits of Norfolk but then a part of Norfolk County.

The disastrous Peninsula Campaign, under the command of General George B. McClellan, had just gotten under way when Lincoln, Secretary of War Edwin M. Stanton, Secretary of the Treasury Salmon P. Chase and Brigadier General Egbert L. Viele left Washington on May 5, 1862, on the Coast Guard cutter *Miami* for Fort Monroe. After an early breakfast the next morning, they visited the ironclad *Monitor*, still battered from its recent and epoch-making encounter with the *Merrimack* (CSS *Virginia*), and then took a trip to the nearby fortifications on the Ripraps.

That night it was decided that Norfolk and Portsmouth must be captured from the Confederates, who had held both since the beginning of the war. After a reconnaissance of the Ocean View beach area by Lincoln and his party, 6,000 troops were ferried across from Fort Monroe on the Old Bay Line steamer *Adelaide*, and the advance on Norfolk was begun.

Although Lincoln was at what is now known as Ocean View as the troops began the southward maneuver, he did not accompany them but returned to Fort Monroe with Stanton to await the result. Secretary Chase accompanied General John E. Wool, however, and was present when Norfolk capitulated to the Federal forces. When the surrender was announced from the steps of the Norfolk Court House (now the MacArthur Memorial), the large crowd that had collected there gave three rousing cheers for Jefferson Davis and three groans for Lincoln and then dispersed.

At 2 a.m. the next day, General Wool rushed into Lincoln's room at Fort Monroe and cried out excitedly, "Norfolk is ours!" Stanton was so jubilant that he hugged the general "in the most enthusiastic manner."

There was no sleeping after that, for by that time large bodies of troops were moving into the newly occupied area, while the skies to the south were aflame with the burning of the Gosport Navy Yard (now the Norfolk Naval Shipyard in Portsmouth) by the retreating Confederates.

Adding to the excitement, the next morning, as Lincoln and his party were about to embark on the steamship *Baltimore* for the return trip to Washington, news arrived that the *Merrimack* had been scuttled near Craney Island. Lincoln and his party then proceeded across Hampton Roads in the same steamer to a point on the Elizabeth River off what is now downtown Norfolk, where they got a closer view of the still-burning navy yard.

Then, after a brief inspection of the river channel to ascertain if it was open for shipping, Lincoln headed back to Washington at the end of what Secretary Chase described as "a brilliant week's campaign by the President."

Lincoln's other visit to the Norfolk area was on February 3, 1865, during what is known as the Hampton Roads Peace Conference, when a last-ditch effort was made to reconcile the Union and the Confederacy. On that occasion, the president, accompanied by Secretary of State William H. Seward, secretly met with three Confederate leaders, Vice President Alexander H. Stephens of Georgia, R.M.T. Hunter of Virginia and Judge John A. Campbell of Alabama.

The conference was held in the cabin of the *River Queen,*

a steamer docked at Fort Monroe. Lincoln expressed his
willingness to recommend to Congress that the Southern slave
owners be compensated for their slaves if the Confederate States
would return to the Union.

The conference was a failure, resulting in three additional
months of bloody fighting, culminated by General Lee's surrender
April 9 at Appomattox.

Even so, the *River Queen* meeting was responsible for a
memorable Lincoln witticism.

Stephens, a tiny man weighing less than 90 pounds, arrived
for the conference muffled up in a heavy overcoat, a scarf and
several shawls. Hoping to break the tension, Lincoln quipped:
"Never have I seen so small a nubbin come out of so much
husk."

Rustling Rebels

The news that General Grant's commissary department, with headquarters near City Point on the James River, had received a magnificent herd of well over 2,400 beef cattle ran like wildfire through the ranks of General Lee's half-starved army encamped around Petersburg.

Even so, the report didn't stop with futile mouthwaterings and wishful thinking, for General Wade Hampton, Lee's dashing, handsome cavalry leader from South Carolina, decided to do something constructive to relieve the hungry Confederate forces that by the late summer of 1864 had been reduced to the scantiest rations.

The resulting action, known in Civil War history as Hampton's Cattle Raid, which took place in mid-September 1864, was one of the most colorful episodes in what diehard rebels still like to refer to over their mint juleps, bourbons and branch water or lowlier beers as the War for Southern Independence.

Learning from Captain George D. Shadburne, the Confederates' chief of scouts, that the lightly guarded herd was quietly grazing in clover fields near Coggins Point in Prince George County, Hampton readily obtained Lee's permission to attempt its capture.

The maneuver was a tricky one as it involved traveling around 50 miles behind the more than 60,000 Union soldiers besieging Petersburg and returning with the captured cattle. But that didn't deter Hampton and his dedicated raiders, to whom a beefsteak by that stage of the war had become a gastronomic rarity.

Shortly after dawn on September 14, 1864, Hampton and around 4,000 cavalrymen, engineers and detachments of horse artillery set out from their encampment to the west of Petersburg.

Proceeding with great secrecy, they crossed the

Blackwater Swamp the next day, and around 5 a.m. swooped down on the Union forces guarding the cattle, taking them completely by surprise.

Two hours later, having defeated the enemy and captured the herd, Hampton's raiding party started back along the same route toward the Confederate lines, driving the mooing and bucking cattle before them.

Recovering from shock, the Federal forces hastily reorganized and attempted to reverse the maneuver and to recapture the herd, but their attacks were weak and disorganized and they were easily beaten back by Hampton's men.

By 9 a.m. on September 17, Hampton was safely back with his bovine prize of war, having lost only 10 men, 47 wounded and four missing in action. Meanwhile, besides the cattle, the raid had netted 304 Federal prisoners and a large quantity of badly needed supplies. Hampton's official report to Lee placed the number of cattle seized at 2,486.

In commenting on his act of derring-do, a Richmond newspaper remarked:

"The Federal commissaries buy beeves of the largest size for the use of their armies in Virginia. The expense and trouble of transportation, which are in proportion to numbers, make this very expedient. The beeves taken in Hampton's late expedition are judged by a London grazier to weigh 800 pounds net. Twenty-four hundred and eighty-six beeves at 800 pounds, would make an aggregate of 1,988,800 pounds, or within a fraction of *two millions of pounds.* This distributed in daily rations of a pound each, would feed 1,000 men for nearly 2,000 days, 10,000 men for 200 days, or 50,000 for 40 days, and so forth. It is a very nice addition to our commissariat, for which we are much obliged to Mr. Grant, and particularly to General Hampton, and his braves."

From the time Grant's herd of cattle was captured by Hampton and his men until the supply was exhausted, the rich odor of frying beefsteak, instead of the usual stench of parched corn, arose from behind the Confederate lines. Besides, the raid was responsible for a telling anecdote that quickly became a part of the saga of the Confederacy.

Soon after the raid, a Yankee and a Confederate picket were standing their posts within hailing distance of each other.

"Say, Reb," the Yankee called out, "why don't you leave

those moth-eaten partners of yours and come over and join us? We'd give you a nice, pretty blue uniform. That old butternut coat you're wearing is sure getting greasy."

"Yeah, I know it's greasy," the Southern boy drawled back, "but don't throw off on it. That grease got on it when I was eatin' that damned tasty beef o' yourn we captured the other day!"

Lincoln Liked "Dixie"

It may come as a shock to most Southerners that "Dixie," the anthem of the Confederacy, was not only one of Abraham Lincoln's favorite tunes, but was also claimed by the Great Emancipator as one of the spoils of war at the close of the Late Unpleasantness. Before letting the cat out of the bag, however, it might be a good idea to include a few words concerning the composer and history of the infectious song, the proper rendition of which is not only capable of eliciting rebel yells from the descendants of those who fought with Marse Robert, but has also been known to have pleasantly raised the blood pressure of the progeny of the boys in blue who gave their all that the Union might be preserved.

Daniel Decatur Emmett, who not only wrote the words and melody of "Dixie" but whose ancestral roots were firmly planted in Virginia, was born on October 29, 1815, in Mount Vernon, Ohio. After joining a circus when he was 20, Emmett abandoned the Big Top in 1842 and organized the Virginia Minstrels, one of the earliest and most popular blackface troupes.

In 1859, Emmett composed "Dixie" as a "walk-around song" for Bryant's Minstrels in New York City, of which he was a member. It became an immediate hit, so much so that it gave rise to a favorite Lincoln anecdote. When the future president first heard it at a New York performance in 1860, he shouted, "Let's have it again" from his box in the theater.

Emmett's infectious song speaks for itself, but the origin of "Dixie," the title by which it is known, is uncertain. During the Civil War or the War Between the States (depending on which side your folks espoused), Southerners generally agreed that it was a corruption of "Mason and Dixon's Line," which divided the free and slave states of the Union. Another version traces the title to $10 bills issued by the Citizens Bank of New Orleans in the 1850s that bore the French word "dix" (i.e., ten) on the reverse side. These banknotes were referred to by Mississippi riverboat gamblers as "Dixies," while the region in which they circulated was known as the "Land of Dixie."

Still another, and highly improbable, tradition derives the name from a kindhearted 18th century New York slave owner named Dixy or Dixie. When his slaves were forced to move South into less congenial circumstances, they traditionally longed for their old home in the North and began to sing of "Dixie Land" as a heaven on earth.

This theory more or less turns the time-honored tradition of the Southland's being a utopia of moonlight, magnolias and mint juleps upside down. Even so, since the last assumption, like the other two, can't be nailed down with any degree of certainty, it might be advisable to abandon the quagmire of speculation for the *terra firma* of solid history.

Soon after its debut, Emmett's song was sung to a wildly cheering audience in New Orleans. Later, on February 18, 1861, it was played as a band selection at the inauguration of Jefferson Davis as president of the Confederacy in Montgomery, Ala. From then on, it became the favorite marching song of the Southern army.

Not to be outdone, a Yankee versifier borrowed the tune of "Dixie" for a set of Northern-slanted verses which, considering the time, made more sense than Emmett's original doggerel. For instance, here is the first verse of the version as it was sung by Union soldiers:

> Away down South in the land of traitors,
> Rattlesnakes and alligators;
> Right away, come away, right away, come away.
> Where cotton's king and men are chattels,
> Union boys will win the battles;
> Right away, come away, right away, come away.
> Then we'll all go down to Dixie, away, away;
> Each Dixie boy must understand
> That he must mind his Uncle Sam,
> Away, Away, we'll all go down to Dixie.

Besides Lincoln's earlier enthusiastic endorsement of "Dixie" in 1860, there are two other contemporary references to his partiality for Emmett's song dating from the end of the war. In 1865, Charles Adolphe Pineton, Marquis de Chambrun, came to the United States from France to make personal observations on the Civil War. After the fall of Petersburg, he accompanied Lincoln to City Point on the James River. After his return, he wrote a private account of his visit which was printed after his death in the January 1893 issue of Scribner's Magazine. In refering to Lincoln's fondness for "Dixie," the marquis recalled:

"We were to leave City Point on Saturday, April 8th. A few hours prior to our leaving, the military band came from the headquarters on board the River Queen. We assembled to hear it. After the performance of several pieces, Mr. Lincoln thought of the 'Marseillaise,' and said to us that he had a great liking for that tune. He ordered it to be played.... He then asked me if I had ever heard 'Dixie,' the rebel patriotic song, to the sound of which all their attacks had been conducted. As I answered in the negative, he added: 'That tune is now Federal property; it belongs to us, and, at any rate, it is good to show the rebels that with us they will be free to hear it again.' He then ordered the somewhat surprised musicians to play it for us."

Of course, unreconstructed Southerners will swear that the French marquis made up his story from whole cloth. So, before we have a second War for Southern Independence on our hands, I'd like to support the marquis' statement of Lincoln's liking for "Dixie" with another quotation. This one comes from the pen of Mrs. Myrta Lockett Avary, a true-blue Virginian and the author of many books on the Civil War that have received the unqualified approval of the United Daughters of the Confederacy. In writing of the days following Appomattox, Mrs. Avary included this personal remembrance:

"General Lee's surrender had been announced and Washington was ablaze with excitement. On April 10, 1865, delirious multitudes surged to the White House, calling the President out for a speech. It was a moment of easy betrayal into words that might widen the breach between sections. He said in his quaint way that he had no speech ready, and concluded humorously: 'I have always thought "Dixie" one of the best tunes I ever heard. I insisted yesterday that we had fairly captured it. I presented the question to the Attorney-General and he gave his opinion that it is our lawful prize. I ask the band to give us a good turn upon it.' In that little speech, he claimed of the South by right of conquest a song — and nothing more."

General Pickett's Friend

One of the lesser-known facts of Virginia history is that there was a close and long-standing personal relationship between Abraham Lincoln and General George Edward Pickett, the gallant Confederate who led the famous charge at the Battle of Gettysburg on July 3, 1863.

The details, for any diehard Southerner who might question this assertion, can easily be found in *Pickett and His Men* by LaSalle Corbell Pickett, the general's second wife, published by Foote & Davis in Atlanta in 1899. Incidentally, the second Mrs. Pickett was a native of Nansemond County, now the city of Suffolk.

Mrs. Pickett's book, which came out 34 years after Appomattox, is not only an accurate and highly readable account of her famous husband and his companions in arms, it is also well written and is regarded by historians as a minor classic of the period of which the Late Unpleasantness was the highlight. Briefly, this is Mrs. Pickett's account of the almost lifelong friendship between the Great Emancipator and the general who is best remembered in history as the man who commanded what is poetically referred to as "the high-water mark of the Confederacy."

Born in Richmond on January 25, 1825, Pickett was a nephew on his mother's side of Andrew Johnston, who, after the Civil War, became a partner in the prestigious Richmond law firm of Johnston, Williams and Boulware. Earlier in his career, however, Johnston was a law partner of Lincoln in Illinois, during which time young Pickett became well acquainted with Old Abe.

Although Pickett's uncle wanted him to become a lawyer, his nephew hankered after a military career, confiding his aspirations to Lincoln. Realizing it was best to humor young Pickett, Lincoln used his political influence with a congressman, John G. Stuart of the Third Illinois District, to secure him an appointment to West Point. Meanwhile, before the nomination was approved, Pickett, who was never a dedicated scholar, made an effort to acquire a smattering of literary polish. This amused Lincoln and prompted him to write to his protege as follows:

"I never encourage deceit, and falsehood, especially if you have got a bad memory, is the *worst* enemy a fellow can have. The fact is truth is your truest friend, no matter what the circumstances are. Notwithstanding this copy-book preamble, my boy, I am inclined to suggest a *little prudence* on your part. You see I have a congenital aversion to failure, and the sudden announcement to your Uncle Andrew of the success of your 'lamp-rubbing' might possibly prevent your passing the severe *physical* examination to which you will be subjected in order to enter the Military Academy. You see, I should like to have a perfect soldier credited to dear old Illinois — no broken bones, scalp wounds, etc. So I think perhaps it might be wise to hand this letter from me, in to your good uncle through his room-window *after* he has had a *comfortable dinner*, and watch its effect from the top of the pigeon-house."

Later, after Pickett had entered West Point, Lincoln sent him this additional advice: "Now, boy, on your march, don't you go and forget the old maxim that 'one drop of honey catches more flies than a half-gallon of gall.' Load your musket with this maxim, and smoke it in your pipe."

Although Pickett graduated from the Military Academy at the foot of his class in 1846, he distinguished himself in the Mexican War and still later in the four bloody years of what unreconstructed rebels still like to refer to as the War for Southern Independence.

Pickett's first wife died in 1851 and he remained a widower until 1862, when he married LaSalle Corbell, who bore him two children. After Pickett died in St. Vincent's Hospital (the forerunner of the present DePaul Hospital) in Norfolk in 1875, his widow, besides writing her husband's biography, was also the author of many fascinating articles on the Lost Cause and its leaders, a practice she continued until her death early in the present century.

From the time of her marriage and for some years thereafter, Mrs. Pickett and her first child, George, lived with the general's uncle, Andrew Johnston, who had returned to Richmond

from Illinois before the Civil War. When Richmond fell early in
April 1865, Mrs. Pickett became increasingly apprehensive that
she, as the wife of one of the South's most distinguished
generals, might be subjected to harsh treatment. Her fears were
groundless, however, for on April 5, 1865, when Lincoln visited
the Confederate capital after it had been taken over by the
Federal forces, a little-known incident took place that runs like a
golden thread through the somber fabric of those troubled times.
Since the episode is one of the highlights in Mrs. Pickett's
account of her husband, it is best to quote her own words.

"Short as was Mr. Lincoln's time when he passed through
Richmond after its surrender, he came to the old Pickett home to
hunt up his friend and former partner, the General's uncle. He
asked about the General himself, and then for the General's wife.
I had seen the carriage and the guard and retinue, but did not
know who the visitors were. In those suspicious times of trouble
and anxiety we did not wait for formal announcements, and we
were following on after the servant who went to answer the bell.
When I heard the caller ask for George Pickett's wife, I came
forward with my baby in my arms.

'I am George Pickett's wife,' I said.
'And I am Abraham Lincoln.'
'The President?'
'No; Abraham Lincoln, George's old friend.'

"Seeing baby's outstretched arms, Mr. Lincoln took him,
and little George opened wide his mouth and gave his father's
friend a dewy baby kiss, seeming to feel with the prescient infant
instinct the tie that binds. As I took my baby back again, Mr.
Lincoln said in that deep and sympathetic voice which was one of
his greatest powers over the hearts of men:

"'Tell your father, the rascal, that I forgive him for the
sake of your mother's smile and your bright eyes.'"

Later, in recalling the same incident and commenting on
Lincoln's dastardly assassination, Mrs. Pickett continued: "I had
sometimes wondered at the General's reverential way of speaking
of President Lincoln, but as I looked up at his honest, earnest
face, and felt the warm clasp of his great, strong hand, I marvelled

no more that all who knew him should love him. When, but a few days later, the wires flashed over the world the tragic message which enveloped our whole nation in mourning, General Pickett said:

"'My God! My God! The South has lost her best friend and protector, the surest, safest hand to guide and steer her through the breakers ahead. Again must we feel the smart of fanaticism!'"

A Hero's Sad End

Any Civil War buff worth his weight in Minie balls knows that Confederate Navy Lieutenant Catesby ap Roger Jones was in command of the CSS *Virginia* (i.e., the former USS *Merrimack*, and better known in history by that name) when it locked horns in Hampton Roads with the USS *Monitor* in the first naval battle between ironclads in 1862. Few, however, are acquainted with Jones' subsequent career which culminated in his murder in Selma, Ala., in June 1877.

To go back a bit, Jones, born in Clark County, Va., in 1821, was a United States naval officer who had resigned his commission in 1861 in order to join the Confederate navy. One of his first duties was to aid in the conversion of the former wooden-hulled *Merrimack* into the ironclad *Virginia* at the Gosport Navy Yard, now the Norfolk Naval Shipyard at Portsmouth.

On March 8, 1862, Jones served as third in command in the *Merrimack*'s initial battle with the Federal fleet in Hampton Roads. In that conflict, Franklin Buchanan, the *Merrimack*'s captain, and his second in command were severely wounded. As a result, Jones commanded the *Merrimack* the next day in its memorable encounter with the *Monitor*, an engagement that impartial historians regard as a drawn battle.

Since Captain Buchanan's injuries prevented him from continuing as the commander of the *Merrimack*, the Confederate government on March 29, 1862, placed the ironclad under the command of Commodore Josiah Tattnall, a 67-year-old former United States naval officer, who, like Jones, had offered his services to the Confederacy. Tattnall named Jones as his second in command.

After the Federal forces recaptured Norfolk on May 10, 1862, the *Merrimack*, at Tattnall's orders, was run aground at Craney Island, and the epoch-making vessel was scuttled and burned. Jones was the last man to leave the *Merrimack*, having remained behind, after the removal of the crew, to light the fires that resulted in the ships's destruction.

The burning of the *Merrimack* drew excited crowds of residents as well as Federal soldiers and sailors along the Elizabeth River and Hampton Roads waterfronts to witness the conflagration. At that time it was recorded that the *Merrimack*'s casemate glowed dull red as its oak and pine foundations disintegrated under the crackling flames. The drama was additionally highlighted when the guns of the doomed ironclad discharged occasionally, sending dull booms across the flame-flickered inky waters.

Finally, after two hours, the *Merrimack*'s death agonies ended at 5 a.m. on the morning of May 11, 1862, when the flames reached the ship's magazine, causing an explosion that shook houses and rattled windowpanes for miles around.

Meanwhile, Tattnall, Jones and the rest of the *Merrimack*'s officers and crew had reached Suffolk, from which they proceeded by train to Richmond. Their arrival was fortuitous, for the subsequent gallantry of the *Merrimack*'s crew at Drury's Bluff, where the ironclad's tattered flags were again hoisted, saved the Confederate capital from being captured on May 15, 1862, from an attack by Federal ships. Incidentally, one of these was the *Monitor*, variously referred to derisively by the Confederates as the "Yankee Notion," the "Tin Can on a Shingle" or the "Cheesebox on a Raft."

True to form, the office-bound Confederate naval brass in Richmond, most of whom had never seen the deck of a ship, roundly condemned Tattnall, Jones and the other officers of the *Merrimack* for destroying the celebrated ironclad, which, because of an inability to maneuver in shallow water, could hardly have escaped being captured by the triumphant Federal forces in the Norfolk area. The hue and cry ended in a court-martial which not only exonerated Tattnall and his fellow officers, but even went further and congratulated them for their fidelity to duty. This decision, a highly unpopular one with the landlubbers in the Confederate Navy Department, was suppressed in the Richmond newspapers.

After his acquittal, Jones was promoted to commander in April 1863. He was ordered to Selma, Ala., to take charge of a government ordnance works and to supervise the completion of the armament of the ironclad *Tennessee.* Two years later, Jones married Gertrude T. Tartt, a Selma girl, and after the fall of the Confederacy he and his wife settled in Selma, where Jones was regarded as one of the city's most distinguished citizens.

Jones' murder in June 1877 was a tragic end to a notable career. By then, he was the father of three sons and three daughters and lived next door to a wholesale grocery merchant named J.A. Harrall. Briefly, the events leading up to Jones' murder are as follows:

One of Jones' sons, Catesby, had battered Harrall's son in a fistfight and had also been impudent to the boy's mother on June 18, 1877. Jones and his wife sent young Catesby to the Harralls' house the next morning to apologize, taking along some apples at his father's bidding as a peace offering. These were rejected by the boy's father, who urged his son to fight young Jones for having bested him the day before. When a relation of Jones' wife saw what was happening, she reported the matter to young Catesby's parents.

Grabbing a cane, ironically made from wood salvaged from the *Merrimack*, Jones went to the Harrall house to demand the reason for his neighbor's truculence. According to a deposition Jones made before his death on June 20, 1877: "I told him (i.e., Harrall) his course was very contemptible, that my boy had come with a note to Mrs. Harrall and to apologize, and he had told his boy to whip him on his own premises. He asked me if I had come there to quarrel with him, and said that he was ready. I told him I did not come to quarrel, but to let him know my opinion of his conduct. I think, I said to him you are a contemptible puppy. He immediately put his hand in his pocket, pulled out his pistol and shot me. I felt a great shock and thought I felt the ball come out behind."

The Jones-Harrall incident caused great consternation in Selma, and after Jones died, Harrall was arrested and tried for murder. Harrall pleaded self-defense, claiming that Jones had threatened to strike him with his cane, and the jury declared him not guilty. By the time of his acquittal, however, Harrall's reputation in Selma, where Jones was highly regarded, was permanently damaged, and he left town shortly afterward.

The Black Colonel

It is appropriate to pay belated tribute to Colonel Joseph Thomas Wilson, the former slave and later African-American Union Army veteran, who edited Norfolk's first black newspaper during the year after the collapse of the Confederacy.

A native of the Norfolk area born in 1836, Wilson escaped from bondage during his early teens and made his way to New Bedford, Mass., where he graduated from the local schools when he was 19. In August 1855 he was hired as a steersman aboard a New England whaler and embarked on a three-year Pacific voyage.

In 1862, while working on a railroad construction project in South America, Wilson learned of the outbreak of the Civil War. Hastening back to New York, he shipped out on a vessel carrying military supplies to the Federal forces at New Orleans.

Upon his arrival, Wilson enlisted as a private in the 2nd Regiment, Louisiana Native Guard Volunteers. Wounded in action, he returned to New Bedford with an honorable discharge. Not content to sit out the war behind the lines, Wilson came to Norfolk, then recently retaken from the Confederates, where he re-enlisted in the Union Army and was assigned to secret service duties in the Elizabeth and James river areas.

Finally, after having taken part in military actions around Petersburg, Wilson was again wounded, so seriously that he was retired permanently from the army. Meanwhile, he had attained the rank of colonel.

At that point, Wilson's journalistic career began. On November 24, 1865, Colonel D.B. White of the 88th Regiment, New York Volunteers, established a Republican-slanted newspaper in Hampton called The True Southerner. Early the next year, the paper was moved to Norfolk and Wilson was made its editor. Using a Franklin-style hand press, Wilson continued to edit and publish the black-oriented paper until late in 1866 when a mob of white hoodlums destroyed his press and the contents of the building in which it was housed.

Fortunately, Wilson escaped to Petersburg, where he became the editor of The Union Republican, a paper owned entirely by white men, many of whom became prominent in state and national politics during the Reconstruction era. By then, Wilson had become so well known in Virginia Republican circles that those in power made efforts to secure him a more lucrative income apart from the precarious pay he earned as a newspaper editor.

In 1869, after The Union Republican ceased publication, he was appointed to the Internal Revenue Service in Richmond as the first gauger (i.e., a customs officer checking bulk goods) in Virginia. Later, Wilson was transferred to the United States Customs Service in Norfolk, where he was listed for several years in the city directories as an "inspector," residing at 300 (E.) Bute Street.

Wilson was a warm and enthusiastic admirer of President Grant and was a presidential elector in 1876 when Rutherford B. Hayes ran successfully for the presidency. Still hankering for a newspaper role, Wilson in 1880 established The American Sentinel in Petersburg, which strongly supported the politics of presidents James A. Garfield and Chester A. Arthur.

Finding his combined duties as a Norfolk customs inspector and Petersburg newspaper editor too strenuous, Wilson resigned his post on The American Sentinel in 1881. Two years later, he was appointed one of a corps of 35 special Internal Revenue agents and was sent to Cincinnati, Ohio. At his request, Wilson was transferred back to Virginia, with headquarters in Richmond. In July 1884, however, Congress halved the number of agents and Wilson was retired.

Despite the fact that his first newspaper, The True Southerner, had been suppressed by mob action in Norfolk. Wilson returned late in 1884 and established The Right Way, a black-slanted Republican newspaper that soon incurred the ire of the city's resurgent Democratic forces. In particular, Wilson's scathing editorials offended Colonel William Lamb, Norfolk's mayor, and George E. Bowden, the collector of customs for the Norfolk District.

According to a biographical sketch of Wilson published in

The Afro-American Press and Its Editors by I. Garland Penn (1891): "By questionable legal proceedings these men (i.e., Lamb and Bowden) got control of the printing material, and in order to stop the publication of the paper, gave it away."

Undeterred, Wilson moved to Richmond in 1885, and organized the highly successful Galilean Fisherman's Insurance Co., an enterprise dedicated to improving the economic lot of Virginia's recently freed black population. Three years later, he was elected a member of the black committee of the Virginia Agricultural, Mechanical and Tobacco Exposition. Later, as its secretary, he met with great success in securing exhibits for what was termed its "Colored Department."

In 1888, Wilson also began the publication in Richmond of The Industrial Day, a periodical "devoted to the industrial idea, as a means of assisting to solve what is termed the race problem."

In the meantime, Wilson had long been active in the local and national affairs of the Grand Army of the Republic, at one time serving as aide de camp to its commander in chief. In 1881, he published a volume of poems, the entire edition of which, consisting of 1,000 copies, sold out in 60 days, with half of the proceeds being donated to the GAR post in Norfolk.

Wilson's chief work, however, came out three years before his death in 1891, and constitutes an invaluable reference work for today's African-Americans who are anxious to prove that their ancestors helped in the creation of the United States of America.

The book is titled *The Black Phalanx: a History of the Negro Soldiers of the United States in the Wars of 1775-1812, 1861-65.* Published in 1888 in Hartford, Conn., this carefully documented volume by a Norfolk-area black man, whose career embraced the roles of slave, sailor, soldier, editor, publisher and businessman, remains a seminal book in American black history.

A Pane in the Apse

Easter Sunday, which fell on April 12 in 1868, dawned peacefully in Hampton Roads. But before the sun set that evening all hell broke loose over a recently installed Confederate-oriented memorial window in Trinity Episcopal Church in Portsmouth.

The window had been presented to the congregation by the Reverend John Henry Wingfield (1798-1871), who had been the rector of the church since 1821. It was intended to be a memorial to nine young Portsmouth men who had lost their lives during the Civil War.

Unfortunately, in composing the inscription for his gift, Wingfield had used wording that gave offense to several U.S. naval officers who had rented pews in the church. Before the offending window was removed, the controversy waxed so hot that the commandant of the Gosport Navy Yard (now the Norfolk Naval Shipyard) received orders from Washington to close the facility if a satisfactory resolution of the matter was not reached.

The first mention of the window controversy appears in a letter from a now-unidentifiable Portsmouth woman to one John C. Ashton. Dated April 14, 1868, it stated:

"Sunday we were all much surprised on going to church to see a magnificent memorial window in the middle-south window. It represents Virginia weeping for her sons. A female figure is leaning on a monument, and inscribed on the monument is: 'To the memory of James G. Hodges, Bristowe B. Gayle, Alexander B. Butt, Frank N. Armistead, William H. Cocke, William H. Bingley, St. Julian Wilson, Stephen A. Cowley, A. Dulaney Forrest, who died during the years 1861 and 1865 in defense of their native State, Virginia, against the invasion by the U.S. forces.'"

To this, the same writer added: "On the upper part of the window is the face of an angel, with outstretched wings, and it is the most beautiful thing I ever saw." This critique was no compliment to the letter-writer's aesthetic taste or that of Portsmouth in general at that time, for the still-surviving window, unlike the glorious examples of medieval stained-glass craftsmanship at Chartres and Canterbury, is a typical example of Victorian ecclesiastical kitsch.

Even so, it was not the garishness of the window that kicked up the trouble. It was the word "invasion" that gravely offended the naval officers present that Easter morning, and it was not long before the fat was in the fire.

Despite the fact that the offended naval officers fanned the controversy by giving up their paid pews, the rest of the Southern-slanted congregation decided to defy any attempt to coerce it into removing the offending window. This is evident from the same letter quoted earlier in which the writer declared, "Not one member of the whole congregation will consent to have one word erased, not if the whole Yankee nation would come to us," adding, "The Yanks themselves may go to 'Old Harry.'"

Having built up that head of Dixie steam, the same writer went on to say, "Some are afraid that the military are carrying such a high hand that there will be an order sent to have it (i.e., the window) taken out, but I reckon they will have to do it themselves for not one of us would lend a hand."

Inserting a personal note, the same writer concluded her resentment against the disgruntled naval officers by declaring, "I really do think that such a miserable set of wretches are not fit to live, and if they die you know where they are only fit to go." To this, she appended, "Cousin Sue was so mad with them this morning that she wanted to have a fist fight and lay hands on all who came in her way. Annie too is piping hot and her tongue is going at a rapid rate."

Meanwhile, the controversy had been taken up by the local press, the brunt of the blame being laid on the "radical leaders in the Navy-yard and in Portsmouth" who were accused of "getting up this excitement for personal and political reasons."

Commenting further on the controversy, another Portsmouth letter writer said, "Our dear old pastor, who presented the window to the church, was so disturbed to think that he had given offense, when his only object was to give a pleasant surprise, that he had a piece of black cloth placed over the inscription. That, again, caused 'Rebel' blood to rise when a young Confederate soldier removed the cloth for which everyone condemned him, as it was placed there by the donor, and the Confederate was not a resident of the place and had no right to meddle with it at all."

Despite the personal sentiments expressed by this letter writer, the majority of the congregation at Trinity secretly applauded the hot-blooded ex-Confederate's action, while the vestry of the church continued to refuse to remove the offending window, feeling that the Navy Yard officers had no right to dictate what ornaments should be placed in their church.

The stalemate continued until the Reverend Joseph Plunkett, the pastor of Portsmouth's Catholic congregation — a man greatly respected for his heroic efforts during the Norfolk-area yellow fever epidemic of 1855 — called on the commandant of the Navy Yard in order to pour oil on the troubled waters. While there, Plunkett was shown an order from the secretary of the Navy stating that if the offending window was not removed by a certain date, the gates of the Navy Yard would be closed, an act that would have brought great economic hardship to the Portsmouth community.

This news caused another Portsmouth letter writer to comment on May 16, 1868. "Of course the throwing of a thousand or more men out of employment was calculated to bring on a horrible state of things, and fears were entertained that the church would be torn down. That would have roused the Southerners, who as it is are much excited, and our dear pastor concluded that the best way to preserve the peace would be to take the window out, but we all hope that the time is not far distant when it can be put back again."

By the time this was written, the window had been removed. In September 1870, however, it was reinstalled. The offending inscription had been discarded and and a new one inserted. It reads: "Given through respect for the Patriotism of the Dead and from sympathy with their bereaved friends by their old pastor on Easter Sunday, 1868".

But the old inscription was not destroyed. Treasured for years by an ardently Southern Portsmouth family, it was pieced together a few years ago and now occupies an honored place in Trinity Church in a frame of its own attached to the sill of the window in which it originally set off a tempest in a teapot.

The Death of Lee

Several eerie happenings marked the death of General Robert E. Lee, the chief hero of the Southern pantheon, which occurred on October 12, 1870.

Lee had been president since September 1865 of Washington College (now Washington and Lee University), where, in the words of Douglas Southall Freeman, his chief biographer, he "had taken a feeble old-fashioned college and had made it a vigorous pioneer in education." During his presidency Lee had also strongly advocated that the defeated Southern states put the past behind them and re-enter the Union without rancor in order that the United States might become a stronger nation.

In words that should shame any diehard Southerner who still hankers for the Confederacy, Lee wrote to an old comrade in arms: "I think it wisest not to keep open the sores of war, but to follow the example of those nations who endeavored to obliterate the marks of civil strife, and to commit to oblivion the feelings it engendered."

Lee had apparently been in excellent health at the time of Appomattox, but his physical condition had rapidly deteriorated in civilian life. Earlier in 1870, in the company of his daughter Agnes, he had taken a Southern trip in an effort to stabilize his condition. At the end of this fruitless excursion he arrived by train in Portsmouth on Saturday, April 30, 1870. He was not only greeted by thousands of his admirers and the booming of cannon, but welcomed by his former aide de camp, Colonel Walter H. Taylor of Norfolk. Taylor accompanied the Lee party across the Elizabeth River to Norfolk where they were the guests of Dr. William Selden, whose home at the southwest corner of Freemason and Botetourt streets remains one of Norfolk's historic landmarks.

While in Norfolk, Lee attended religious services at both Christ Church and St. Paul's Church in the downtown area. Also, while he was Dr. Selden's guest he was visited by hundreds of his former companions in arms who seized the opportunity to greet their old commander once more. On May 4, 1870, Lee and his daughter boarded a steamer for Lower Brandon Plantation on the James River where they stayed briefly with the Harrison family before heading back to Lexington.

Once there, Lee resumed his college duties, but everyone was aware that the man who had by then gained even the admiration of all well-disposed Northerners for his nobility in defeat was old at 63. Still, no appreciable change took place until September 28, 1870. That day, as Lee left his office, he was approached by Percy Davidson, a college sophomore, who had a small photograph of the general which he hoped Lee would autograph for his sweetheart. Sensing that Lee was anxious to get home, Davidson offered to come back later, but Lee replied, "No, I will go back and do it now." He then returned to his office and autographed the photograph. It was the last time he was ever to sign his name.

Lee then walked home for his noonday dinner, after which he prepared to attend a vestry meeting at Lexington's Grace Episcopal Church. As a heavy downpour had set in, he put on his old military cape for greater protection. Before leaving the President's House, however, he commented wryly on the dolorous tune, the "Funeral March" from Mendelssohn's "Songs Without Words," which his daughter Agnes was endeavoring to master at the piano.

The meeting in the damp, unheated church was a long one and was only briefly enlivened when Lee recounted several anecdotes concerning Chief Justice John Marshall and Bishop William Meade. Then, around 7 p.m., he walked home "in such a rain as had fallen that night when the army had crossed the Potomac in retreat from Gettysburg." When he arrived, it was noted that he was unwell, and when he took his accustomed place at the head of the supper table and attempted to say grace he was unable to do so.

Doctors were immediately summoned, while the dining room was hastily converted into a downstairs bedroom to accommodate the gravely ill man. Meanwhile, the news of his seizure leaked out and soon the wires were regularly reporting his condition. Even though some were hopeful of a change, others were not so sanguine, and by September 29, 1870, the Standard, Disraeli's newspaper in London, had begun to compile a review of Lee's career to be included in his shortly anticipated obituary.

At that point, while the beloved Southern leader struggled with his last enemy, strange things began to happen. First, a heavy portrait of Lee fell from its accustomed place on the wall. Even though Mrs. Lee refused to be superstitious about it, people who learned of the incident began to whisper that a fallen portrait was a certain portent of the death of the subject. Then something even more spectacular took place. For several nights the skies north of Lexington were brilliantly illuminated with a display of the aurora borealis. This caused one Lexington matron to take down her copy of *The Lays of the Scottish Cavaliers* and point significantly to this quatrain from the poem "Edinburgh After Flodden":

> All night long the northern streamers
> Shot across the trembling sky:
> Fearful lights that never beckon
> Save when kings or heroes die.

From then on Lee's condition worsened, and the doctors knew it was only a matter of time before he would die. On one occasion, one of his physicians tried to arouse his interest by telling him that Traveller, his beloved horse, had been too long in the stable and needed exercise. But Traveller's master only responded by shaking his head and pointing upward. Finally, at 9:30 on the morning of October 12, 1870, Lee uttered his last words, "Strike the tent!" Then the hero of the Southland died quietly, after which the word passed quickly from his home to the campus and then to Lexington, where church bells were soon tolling.

Lexington had been practically isolated by the recent rains and flooded streams, and the news did not reach Richmond and the rest of the country until late that evening.

No suitable coffin could be found in which to bury Lee's body. According to an appendix in the fourth volume of Freeman's life of Lee, three caskets had been ordered by a Lexington undertaker from Richmond a short time before Lee's death. Before these could be removed from the town's packet landing where they had been delivered, however, they had been washed away by the unprecedented flooding.

Fortunately two boys discovered one of the coffins washed up on the shore of the Maury River. As it was undamaged, it was used for Lee's body although it was too short for him. For that reason, the general, dressed in dark civilian clothing, was buried without shoes. Meanwhile, before Lee's body was prepared for burial, a plaster death mask was made.

The day of Lee's funeral on October 15, 1870, was brilliantly clear, and despite the washed-out bridges and mired roads the service was attended by hundreds of Lee's former soldiers. Colonel Taylor of Norfolk accompanied the family to the college chapel for the last rites, after which the general's body was placed in a vault created for the coffin that had been rescued by the two boys from the rampaging river. Then all present joined in the singing of the hymn "How Firm a Foundation Ye Saints of the Lord" and Lee's simple burial rites were over.

Trampled by History

The old saying "Truth is stranger than fiction" was eerily verified by three episodes in the life of Wilmer McLean (1815-82), whose two Virginia country homes played stellar roles in the Civil War.

Not only was McLean's farmhouse on Bull Run Creek near Manassas Junction in Northern Virginia in the midst of the fighting during the first and second Battles of Bull Run (also known as First and Second Manassas), it was in the parlor of his later home at Appomattox Court House on April 9, 1865, that General Robert E. Lee surrendered the Army of Northern Virginia to General Ulysses S. Grant, the commander of the victorious Union Army of the Potomac.

McLean, whose Scottish forebears had come to Virginia from the island of Iona, one of the Inner Hebrides, was born in Alexandria where he accumulated a comfortable fortune in the wholesale and retail grocery business during his earlier years.

A lover of quiet country living, McLean used some of his savings after retirement to acquire a 1,400-acre estate on Bull Run about 30 miles southwest of Washington where he prospered for a time as a farmer.

The outbreak of the Civil War changed McLean's bucolic existence, however, for he soon found himself unexpectedly involved in the conflict. At that time the sleepy little rural community to which McLean, an avowed pacifist, had retired suddenly became a focal point in the four-year bloody struggle that is still referred to in unreconstructed circles as The War for Southern Independence.

In the first Battle of Bull Run (First Manassas), on July 21, 1861, Union forces, confident of an easy triumph that would enable them to push on to Richmond, were initially successful. But the stand of the Confederate brigade led by General Thomas J. Jackson, which won him the nickname of "Stonewall," and the arrival of reinforcements turned the apparent Union victory into a rout.

The second Battle of Bull Run (Second Manassas), fought on August 30, 1862, ended in defeat again for the Union.

During the first engagement, McLean's house was in the direct line of fire and was commandeered as a hospital and a morgue. At one point during the first Battle of Bull Run, McLean's house was temporarily the headquarters of Confederate General Pierre Gustave Toutant Beauregard.

On that occasion, according to the memoirs of Confederate Brigadier General Edward Porter Alexander (1835-1910), a family connection of McLean's, "The first hostile shot which I ever saw fired was aimed at the house (McLean's), and a third or fourth went through its kitchen, where our servants were cooking dinner for the headquarters staff."

In an effort to remove his family to a place of relative safety where, according to his own words, "the sound of no battle would ever reach," McLean sold his Northern Virginia property and bought a handsome brick house at Appomattox Court House in Southside Virginia. There he lived quietly until the fall of Petersburg again brought the horrors of war to his doorstep.

On April 2-3, 1865, General Lee evacuated Petersburg. Three days later he fought off a Union threat at Sayler's Creek, while on April 7 he beat off another attack at Farmville. On the night of April 8, however, the outnumbered Confederates saw the Union campfires blazing all around them at Appomattox, and the realization that the enemy was closing in on them became painfully apparent.

On the morning of April 9, 1865, which was Palm Sunday, General Lee put on a new gold-braided uniform, buckled on his sword, and after pulling on his gloves informed his staff, "I am going to see General Grant." Sending his flag of truce on ahead, Lee rode into the village of Appomattox at 1 p.m., at which time Wilmer McLean's home again became a focal point in history.

Shortly afterward, the parlor of the McLean House became the backdrop for an epochal decision by Lee. Seeing it was useless to struggle further against overwhelming odds, he surrendered the Army of Northern Virginia to Grant, whose generous terms to his defeated antagonist and his hard-fighting men will always serve as a reminder of the Union general's magnanimity.

All of which recalls another Appomattox story that incidentally reveals Lee's quiet sense of humor. One of the myths that survived long after the war was that the surrender took place under an apple tree.

"You met under an apple tree, did you not, general?" Lee was asked once as he was recollecting the event.

"No, sir, we did not," Lee replied. "We met in Mrs. McLean's parlor. If there was an apple tree there, I did not see it."

Even so, the general's denial fell on deaf ears for a long time and the orchards around Appomattox were practically denuded by enterprising veterans who sold thousands of "Surrender Tree splinters" all over the country as souvenirs of what supposedly took place on that far-off Palm Sunday in 1865.

As to McLean's reaction to what had taken place, the memoirs of his kinsman, Brigadier General Alexander, which was quoted earlier, have this to say: "I had not seen or heard of McLean for years, when the day after the surrender, I met him at Appomattox Court-house, and asked with some surprise what he was doing there.

"He replied, with much indignation: 'What are you doing here? These armies tore my place on Bull Run all to pieces, and kept running over it backward and forward till no man could live there, so I just sold out and came here, two hundred miles away, hoping I should never see a soldier again. And now, just look around you! Not a fence-rail is left on the place, the last guns trampled down all my crops, and Lee surrenders to Grant in my house.'"

To this, Alexander later added: "McLean was so indignant that I felt bound to apologize for our coming back, and to throw all the blame for it upon the gentlemen on the other side."

After Lee's historic surrender in his Appomattox Court House home, McLean did not long remain in Southside Virginia. When peace was declared, he sold his property there and returned to Alexandria where he subsequently served as a United States customs official.

He died in Alexandria in June 1882, and is buried in St. Paul's Episcopal Cemetery there where his tombstone makes no mention of the important role that he and his homes played during the Civil War.

The Last Battle

Contrary to popular belief, the Civil War did not end in Virginia with the surrender of General Robert E. Lee to General Ulysses S. Grant in the parlor of the McLean House at Appomattox Court House on Palm Sunday, April 9, 1865. The four years of bloody fratricidal struggle ended in tragi-comedy on May 23 of the same year in a swampy country graveyard five miles from Floyd, Va.

At that time three defiant and drunken paroled Confederate soldiers in their twenties were felled by a synchronized volley fired by around 500 Union troops under the command of Brigadier General George Stoneman (1822-94). Stoneman not only served the Federal cause throughout the war, during which time he was engaged in Sherman's well-publicized Atlanta campaign, but ended his career as governor of California from 1883 to 1887.

I discovered the almost unbelievable episode concerning the three disgruntled Confederates in a one-paragraph account in *The People's Almanac No. 2,* compiled by David Wallechinsky and Irving Wallace in 1978, headed "The Last Soldiers Killed in the Civil War." Further research led me to Volume XXI of the *Southern Historical Society Papers* which contained a detailed account of the episode reprinted from the Richmond (Va.) Times for March 5, 1893. It is from this expanded source that I have taken the details for this column.

Before I give an account of this last *beau geste* of the Confederacy, it might be a good idea to include a brief resume of the events that culminated in the harebrained decision of the three men to take on an entire Union army rather than turn their backs on their belief in Southern independence, the cause they had espoused for four years with grim determination.

Until the last months of the war, Floyd and Wythe counties had been spared the horrors of invasion and pillage. In

March 1865, however, General Stoneman was ordered to take over these two remote western Virginia communities. After the capture of Wytheville and Lynchburg, the area was ravaged so thoroughly by Federal cavalry that a secret society was organized to retaliate against further Union depredations.

Most of the members of the cabal were young men who had taken no part in the war, though it included rebel soldiers home on leave. After the surrender at Appomattox, membership in the society was augmented by many of Lee's former soldiers who had been paroled and permitted to return to their homes in Floyd and Wythe counties. Among these were three particularly embittered Confederate privates named William Bordunix, John McMasters and Owen Lewis. Their fiery refusal to accept Lee's decision to surrender, bolstered by the consumption of a good deal of hard liquor, contributed greatly to plans already under way to wreak a suitable revenge on Stoneman's army of occupation.

In mid-May 1865, matters came to a head when it was learned that Stoneman and the army under his command would shortly pass through Floyd County en route to Washington. By May 18, 1865, scouts of the secret society reported that Stoneman, with 6,000 cavalrymen, 10,000 infantrymen and 23 guns, had begun a 100-mile march over the mountains toward the Virginia and Tennessee Railroad terminal at Christiansburg to entrain for the national capital.

Fearing that any overt resistance by the secret society to impede the movement of the Federal forces would bring on serious retaliation, wiser and older heads in the community persuaded all but Bordunix, McMasters and Lewis to abandon plans to ambush Stoneman's forces.

Undaunted, Bordunix, McMasters and Lewis excoriated those who had vowed earlier to make a last stand with them. Keyed up with drink and a sense of betrayal, the three entered the town of Floyd, where "with oaths (they) boasted that they would exterminate the whole of Stoneman's army."

Heading its account "The Last Blood Shed/Three Virginians Who Battled Against a Whole Army" with the subhead "Buried Where They Fell Dead, A Mad Scheme to Wreak Vengeance, They Sold Their Lives Dearly," this is how the Richmond Times recounted the incident: "In another hour the head of the army appeared at the outskirts of the village. By this time the three men were crazed by liquor, and in marching order, with Bordunix in the lead, acting as commander, boldly advanced to meet the great army of Stoneman with as little fear as did David to battle with the mighty hosts of the Philistines. When within a stone throw of the front of the column they entered a field grown with bushes. The march of the three men was watched with interest by the inhabitants of the town, who had turned out in full force to see the army pass. They had no idea that the boasts of the men were more than idle threats.

"After entering the field Bordunix halted his followers, and greatly to the amusement of the Union troops, put them through drill. They were greeted with good-natured cries from the soldiers, giving the rebel war-cry of 'Yip, yip, yah!' Finally, Bordunix gave the order to aim and then to fire, at the same time suiting the action to the word. The amazement of the Unionists can be imagined when two of their number fell seriously wounded.

"Before they had fully recovered from their surprise another volley was fired, wounding others. The three men hastily retreated. The town was searched, but they were not found, as they had gone further down the road. The army moved forward, and a mile from town was again fired upon, this time from ambush. The order was given to capture them alive, and they were charged by at least five hundred men, but were not taken, as they apparently knew the rough country well.

"Another mile, and three more Union soldiers fell under their aim. Two miles further on three others fell out of the ranks, and were carried to the road to await the arrival of the ambulance. The three avengers hastened forward, and found concealment in a graveyard beside the highway. Here they waited again for Stoneman's army."

After that, the last active resistance of the Confederacy advanced quickly to its tragic climax. "The troops were ordered to fire if another assault was made," the newspaper account concluded. "They advanced nervously for the fifth time. Suddenly the crack of three rifles was heard, and the roar of 500 muskets answered it. The mad Virginians fell riddled with bullets, and were buried where they fell. Theirs was the last blood shed in the war."